CURRENCY CONVERS

This chart provides a scale of prices converted from GB pounds, based on a conversion rate of $1.45 to the pound

£1	$1.45
£5	$7.25
£10	$14.50
£20	$29.00
£25	$36.25
£50	$72.50
£75	$108.75
£100	$145.00
£125	$181.25
£150	$217.50
£175	$253.75
£200	$290.00
£250	$362.50
£300	$435.00
£400	$580.00
£500	$725.00
£750	$1,087.50
£1,000	$1,450.00
£2,000	$2,900.00
£5,000	$7,250.00
£7,500	$10,875.00
£10,000	$14,500.00
£20,000	$29,000.00
£30,000	$43,500.00
£40,000	$58,000.00
£50,000	$72,500.00
£100,000	$145,000.00

ANTIQUES FURNITURE

THIS IS A CARLTON BOOK

This edition published by Carlton Books Ltd 2002
20 Mortimer Street
London
W1T 3JW

ISBN 1 84222 525 1

Printed and bound in Italy

ANTIQUES FURNITURE

MARTIN MILLER

CARLTON BOOKS

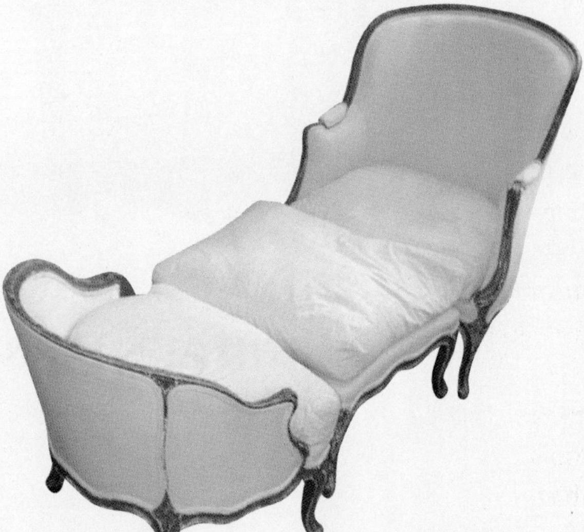

CONTENTS

ACKNOWLEDGEMENTS

GENERAL EDITOR

Martin Miller

EDITORS

Simon Blake

Marianne Blake

Abigail Zoe Martin

Peter Blake

EDITORIAL CO-ORDINATORS

Marianne Blake

Abigail Zoe Martin

PHOTOGRAPHIC/PRODUCTION CO-ORDINATOR

Marianne Blake

PHOTOGRAPHERS

Abigail Zoe Martin

James Beam Van Etten

Anna Malni

Chris Smailes

How to Use This Book

by MARTIN MILLER

Due to the phenomenal success of my annual *Antiques Source Book*, we are now producing a series of specialist handbooks, each concentrating on a specific area of antique buying and collecting.

Antiques: Furniture is a full-colour furniture retail price guide. The reason that it stands out from other antique price guides is that we have used retailers, rather than auction houses, as our sources of information. Many of the items in this book are for sale at the time of going to press and a number, certainly some of the more arcane, will remain so for the lifespan of the book. A reputable and experienced dealer's assessment of the price of an antique is at least as reliable – and usually a great deal more reasoned – than a price achieved at auction, and so even when the item you wish to purchase from the book turns out to have been sold, you have a reliable guide to the price you should pay when you happen upon another.

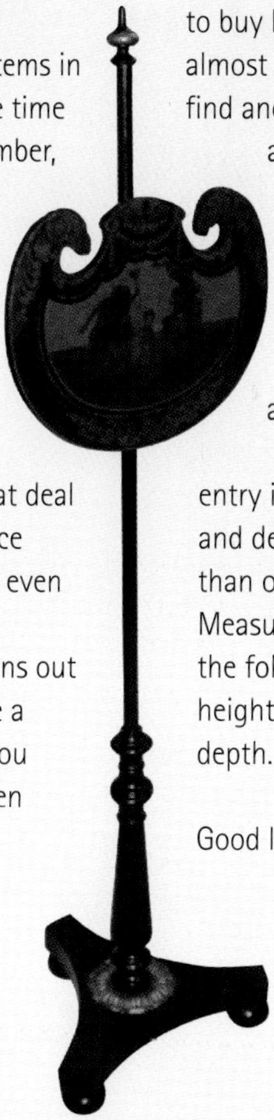

Should you spot something in this book that you wish to buy, simply note the dealer reference to the bottom right of the entry and look up the dealer's full name and details in the Directory of Dealers section at the back of the book. You can telephone, fax and, in many cases, visit the dealer's website. All the dealers who have helped us with the book will be happy to assist you and, if the piece you wish to buy has already been sold, they will almost certainly be able to help you find another. Should you wish to sell an item of furniture, the relevant section and dealer reference will again be of help, but do not expect to be offered the same price at which the dealer is selling. We all have to make a living!

The price shown against an entry is per item, unless the heading and description refer only to more than one item, a set or a pair. Measurements are always given in the following order, as relevant: height or length; width or diameter; depth.

Good luck and good hunting!

Introduction

The market for antique furniture goes from strength to strength and is spreading across the world

The most used antiques of them all and, obviously, a vast field of study, antique furniture varies considerably in style depending on the period and the country in which it was made. Most collectors tend to concentrate on one area or one period, bookcases and cabinets, for instance, or Victorian furniture.

Fakes, reproductions and updated pieces abound in this field more than any other, and it is important to be able to tell when a piece is 'right'.

A methodical approach to examination is important to be able to judge whether there has been any restoration – or whether distressing is evident in a place which would not have been distressed during the course of natural usage or wear.

There is no substitute for experience. The more used you are to handling and examining the real thing, the more likely you are to identify the 'wrong' one.

The best reason for buying a piece of furniture is a genuine liking for it, so there is some satisfaction and pleasure in the possession in any event. However, the better informed you are about the main buying criteria – style, materials, method of construction, period, manufacturer – the more likely you are to make a wise purchase and the more you will enjoy the experience of owning it.

The traditional view about furniture is that the discerning buyer would only consider pieces made between the seventeenth and the late eighteenth century.

As these limitations have now been lifted the future for furniture looks extremely bright, for antiques right up to modern-day designer pieces. This can be seen by the current fashion among the discerning collector or interior designer for snapping up furniture made by art students and studios across the world.

Similarly, as new materials suitable for furniture-making are developed and with the advent of mass production, pieces by Conran and Philip Starck are becoming collectable, however, for the designer and cabinet-maker wood in its natural state will never lose its appeal.

As a result of this, antique furniture dealers and their shops are as varied as the items they sell, and Martin Miller wishes you great fun and success on the antiques trail.

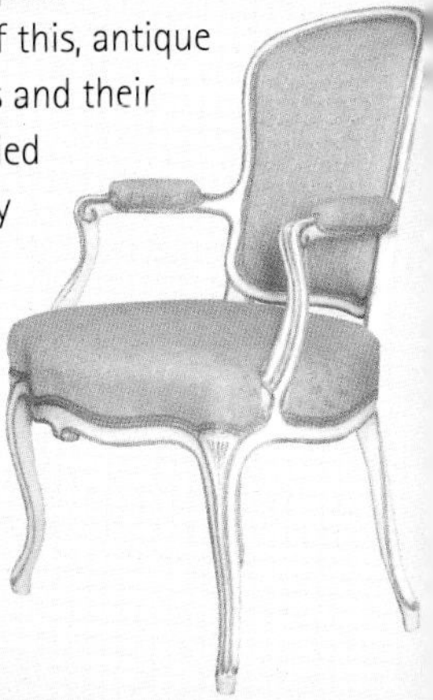

Beds

Louis XVI Bed
• *circa 1880 (1774–93)*
A mahogany Louis XVI-style bed with brass moulding and mounts.
• £1,550 • Old Cinema

Chippendale Bed
• *18th century*
A Chippendale mahogany bed reconstructed to current size with modern cream silk canopy insert.
• *width 1.82m*
• £6,500 • Mora & Upham

Walnut Bed
• *1860*
Walnut Louis XV-style bed, with elaborately carved and scrolled head and footboard, standing on scrolled splayed feet.
• *width 1.8m*
• £6,250 • Sleeping Beauty

French Walnut Bedhead
• *1860*
French walnut, Louis Philipe bedhead, with carved moulded arched headboard, foliate design and panelling, on bun feet.
• *width 1.5m*
• £5,750 • Sleeping Beauty

Oak Bedroom Suite
• *circa 1785*
A French suite consisting of bed, bedside table, washstand, armoire, chest and much more.
• £25,000 • Sleeping Beauty

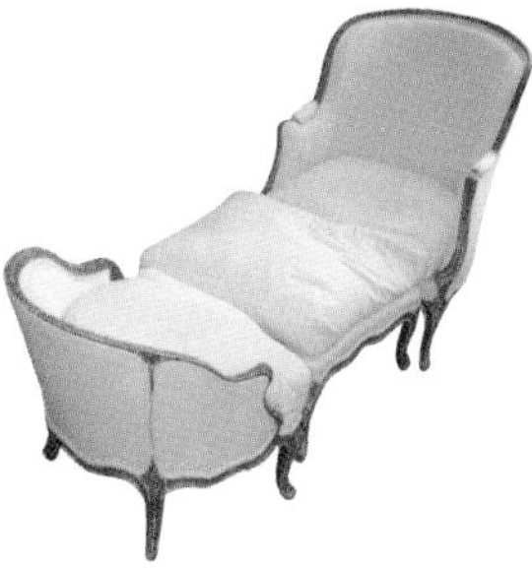

Expert Tips

Four-poster beds became unfashionable in the 18th and 19th centuries, and many were dismantled. Most of the beds on the market today are made up from the discards.

Louis XV Walnut Bed
• *circa 1890*
A five-foot Louis XV solid walnut bed. Heavily carved with swags and roses.
• £2,250 • Sleeping Beauty

Italian Inlaid Bedheads
• *circa 1880*
Pair of unusual Italian hand-painted iron bedheads, inlaid with mother of pearl, standing on tapered legs.
• *width 90cm*
• £4,500 • Sleeping Beauty

Louis XV Daybed
• *1870*
Louis XV-style daybed with painted and parcel-gilt frame and shell and leaf carving, on scrolled cabriole legs.
• *length 2.42m*
• £6,500 • O.F. Wilson

Louis XV-Style Suite ▲

- ***circa* 1890**

Painted French bedroom suite of dressing table, armoire and bedside table with original marble.

- £12,000 • **Sleeping Beauty**

Four-Poster Bed ▲

- ***18th century***

A four-poster carved bed with twisted columns.

- *height 2.16m*
- £2,450 • **Drummonds**

Louis XV-Style Bed ▼

- ***circa* 1890**

A rare six-foot wide walnut-framed bed with heavily carved roses on footboard.

- *width 1.78m*
- £6,500 • **Sleeping Beauty**

French Renaissance-Style Bed ►

- ***circa* 1860**

Ebonised four-poster bedstead with heavily carved turned posts with canopy and carved footboard.

- *length 1.9m*
- £8,500 • **Sleeping Beauty**

Expert Tips

Plaques bearing a maker's name are a mark of quality in brass beds. Among these are Maple and Co, Heal and Son and R. W. Winfield; the latter made beds for royal households and the plaque bears a coat-of-arms.

French Bed ▲

- ***circa* 1885**

A French Chapeau Gendarme with ornate brasswork and large castings.

- *length 1.5m*
- £1,895 • **Sleeping Beauty**

Victorian Brass Bed ▼

- ***circa* 1860**

An early Victorian all-brass bedstead with barley-twist posts.

- *length 2.2m*
- £18,000 • **Sleeping Beauty**

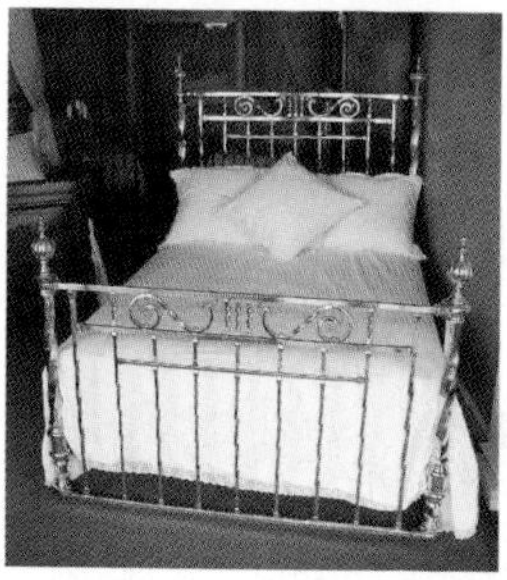

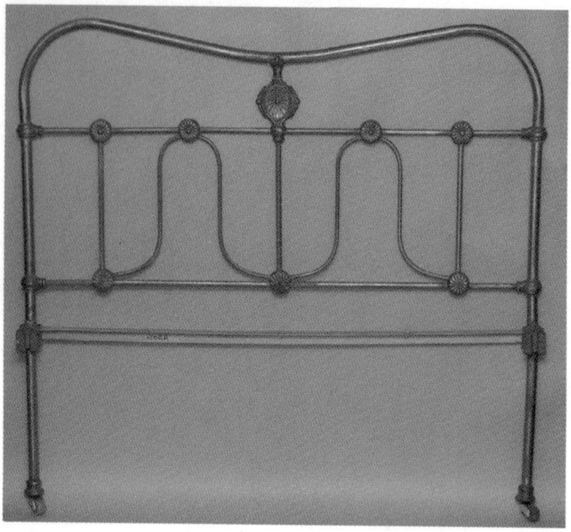

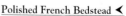

Polished French Bedstead ◄

- ***circa* 1870**

A small, double polished bedstead with floral rosettes.

- *height 1.1m*
- £500 • **After Noah**

Brass Bedstead

- *1860*

Victorian brass bedstead with turned posts, ornate finials and scrolled decoration.

- *width 1.5m*
- £18,000 • **Sleeping Beauty**

Carved Walnut Bed

- *1885*

French walnut Louis XVI-style bed, with finely carved floral swags and garlands to the bedhead and footboard.

- *width 1.6m*
- £6,500 • **Sleeping Beauty**

Expert Tips

When purchasing bedheads and ends make sure that the supporting rods fit correctly as there is nothing worse than an unsteady bed. With brass bedheads, establish whether it is solid brass or a thin leaf of brass over an iron frame as brass leaf often cracks, exposing the iron frame underneath, and looks extremely unsightly.

Louis XVI Bergère-Style Bed

- *circa 1880*

A Louis XVI bergère-style bow fronted bed with carved walnut frame and central oval floral design.

- *width 1.5m*
- £6,250 • **Sleeping Beauty**

Wrought-Iron Bed

- *1860*

Unusual Victorian wrought-iron bedstead incorporating an arched design, on turned legs.

- *width 1.5m*
- £4,000 • **Sleeping Beauty**

Empire Bed

- *1860*

French Second Empire heavily carved and ebonised four-poster bed, with scrolled broken pediment and turned posts.

- *width 1.5m*
- £8,500 • **Sleeping Beauty**

Bergère-Style Bed

- *1885*

French bergère Louis XVI-style bed with moulded headboard and fluted posts, standing on turned feet.

- *width 1.5m*
- £3,500 • **Sleeping Beauty**

Bonheurs du Jour

Lady's Desk

- *circa 1870*

A 19th-century English bonheur du jour in lacquered bamboo, with splayed legs on an "H"-frame stretcher.

- *height 1.24m (to top)*
- £1,250 • **North West 8**

Make-Up Table

- *circa 1910*

An Edwardian lady's make-up table in rosewood, with inlay, two drawers and two side cabinets, the whole on tapered legs with castors.

- *height 88cm*
- £750 • **Antiques Pavilion**

Burr-Walnut Bonheur du Jour

- *circa 1860*

A Victorian burr-walnut bonheur du jour with boxwood inlay, gilt ormolu mounts and cabriole legs. The interior in rosewood with leather inset to the writing surface. Shows three mirrors.

- *height 1.42m*
- £3,800 • **Judy Fox**

Walnut Bonheur du Jour

- *circa 1860*

An English marquetry inlaid walnut bonheur du jour with ornately carved mounts and cabriole legs.

- *height 1.2m*
- £3,800 • **Furniture Vault**

Burr Walnut Bonheur

- *circa 1870*

Boxwood seaweed inlay with ormolu mounts and gallery mirror.

- *height 1.4m*
- £3,800 • **Judy Fox**

Inlaid Bonheur

- *circa 1860*

A two-drawer, Victorian bonheur du jour, the upper section with cupboard doors inlaid with floral decoration and pillared mirror.

- *height 80cm*
- £1,100 • **Tower Bridge**

Louis XV-Style Bonheur du Jour

• *late 19th century*
Kingwood and crossbanded bonheur du jour in the Louis XV-style, applied with gilt metal mounts and Sèvres-style porcelain plaques. The stepped superstructure with a three-quarter gallery and marble top above a panelled door inset with a plaque depicting courtly lovers, and four short drawers. The rectangular galleried top above a frieze drawer with similar applied decoration, on slender cabriole legs and scroll feet with sabots.
• *117cm x 92cm x 51cm*
• £15,000 • **Emanouel**

Rosewood Bonheur du Jour

• *circa 1820*
Regency rosewood bonheur du jour, with satinwood inlay and mirrored back panel, flanked by cupboards with oval satinwood panels, standing on straight square tapering legs.
• *105cm x 90cm x 46cm*
• £2,995 • **Harpur Deardren**

Satinwood Bijouterie

• *circa 1870*
Satinwood bijouterie with fine floral design, standing on slender tapered legs, with scrolled stretcher.
• *height 84cm*
• £6,500 • **Butchoff Antiques**

Coromandel Lady's Necessaire

• *1920–30*
A coromandel lady's necessaire with fitted interior containing original bottles and pull-out flaps, and a stretcher below. Standing on squared tapered legs on splayed feet.
• *72cm x 25cm*
• £3,450 • **Great Grooms**

Mahogany and Satinwood Bonheur du Jour

• *1850*
Mahogany and satinwood bonheur du jour with a raised pierced gallery, with four small drawers and a leather writing top, with two small drawers below, raised on reeded tapered legs.
• *95cm x 81cm x 48cm*
• £5,950 • **Ashcombe House**

English Regency Bonheur du Jour

• *1815*
Outstanding and rare Regency coromandel bonheur du jour. This is a fine and elegant example of English Regency furniture.
• *119cm x 70cm x 67cm/extended*
• £14,500 • **Freshfords**

Expert Tips

When inspecting furniture it is a good idea to start with the legs as these are often the first part to get damaged and need replacement.

Bookcases

Chippendale Bookcase

- *circa 1900*

In mahogany with swan-neck pedament inscribed "T. Wilson, 66 Great Queen St, London".

- *height 2.42m*
- £4,900 • **Furniture Vault**

Bureau Bookcase

- *circa 1790*

George III mahogany with brass fittings and a leather-fitted desk.

- *height 2.27m*
- £4,800 • **Chris Newland**

Breakfront Bookcase

- *circa 1810*

Mahogany with astragal-glazed doors, cupboard and drawers.

- *height 2.52m*
- £24,500 • **Chambers**

Rosewood Bookcase

- *circa 1830*

A late-Regency open bookcase with carved pilasters and three adjustable shelves.

- *height 1.07m*
- £2,950 • **M. J. Bowdery**

Secretaire Chest

- *19th century*

A mahogany secretaire chest with swan-neck pediment.

- *height 2.04m*
- £1,450 • **Castlegate**

Breakfront Bookcase

- *circa 1835*

Flame mahogany bookcase with unusual glazed upper doors.

- *height 1.92m*
- £16,500 • **Paul Andrews**

Biedermeier Bookcase

• *circa 1900*
Swedish birchwood bookcase in the Biedermeier style with gilt mounts, ebonised pillars and a moulded top.
• *height 1.24m*
• £4,500 • **Rupert Cavendish**

Victorian Bookcase

• *circa 1850*
A two-door glazed secretaire bookcase in mahogany with architectural pillars.
• *height 2.22m*
• £2,250 • **Castlegate**

Secretaire Bookcase

• *circa 1830*
William IV bookcase set in mahogany with brass fittings.
• *height 2.1m*
• £4,250 • **F. Beck**

Bureau Bookcase

• *circa 1790*
A simple oak bureau bookcase with four graduating drawers and two pull-out candle holders.
• *height 2.15m*
• £3,800 • **Chris Newland**

Oak Bookcase

• *circa 1910*
An oak bookcase originally from a post office, more lately from an author's library.
• *height 1.33m*
• £1,450 • **Julia Bennet**

Breakfronted Bookcase

• *circa 1810*
One of a pair of bookcases, with glazed doors above moulded double doors.
• *height 2.36m*
• £24,500 • **Chambers**

Oak Bookcase

- ***19th century***

Light oak bookcase with glazed doors above two drawers and two doors, all with original mounts.

- *height 2.25m*
- **£1,295** • **Old Cinema**

Walnut Bookcase

- ***19th century***

Three-tiered bookcase with Gothic bars and two drawers.

- *height 1.96m*
- **£850** • **Tower Bridge**

Breakfront Bookcase

- ***circa 1825***

A George IV figured mahogany breakfront bookcase.

- *height 2.52m*
- **£100,000** • **Norman Adams**

Open Bookcase

- ***circa 1820***

Simulated rosewood bookcase with two shelves on turned feet and brass castors.

- *height 1.3m*
- **£1,650** • **M. J. Bowdery**

Breakfront Bookcase

- ***circa 1830***

A 19th-century English Gothic country house burr elm and amboyna breakfront bookcase with cabinet.

- *height 1.17m*
- **£9,800** • **Luther & Goodwin**

Globe Werniker

- ***circa 1915***

Six-stack, oak Globe Werniker bookcase with lifting glass panels.

- *height 2m*
- **£950** • **Oola Boola**

Mahogany Bookcase ➤

• *circa* **1900**
Fine astragal-glazed doors raised on ogee bracket feet.
• *height 99cm*
• £780 • Ranby Hall

Secretaire Bookcase ▲

• *circa* **1795**
A rare small Sheraton-period secretaire in satinwood and coromandel.
• *height 1.94m*
• £60,000 • Norman Adams

George III Bookcase ➤

• *circa* **1800**
Bookcase with lion-shaped brass handles. Bureau with three graduating drawers, ivory handles.
• *height 2.27m*
• £4,200 • Chris Newland

Mahogany Bookcase ▲

• *circa* **1820**
Waterfall mahogany bookcase.
• *height 1.92m*
• £6,000 • T. Morse

Mahogany Bookcase ▲

• *circa* **1900**
A mahogany bookcase with two glazed-over two-panelled doors.
• *height 2.3m*
• £2,200 • Fulham

Breakfront Bookcase ▼

• *circa* **1870**
A very fine coromandel breakfront bookcase, with four glazed doors.
• *height 2.65m*
• £22,000 • Butchoff

Edwardian Revolving Bookcase

• ***1901–10***

An Edwardian mahogany revolving bookcase of small proportions, on a stand with cabriole legs and shelf.

• *84cm x 40cm*

• **£1,450** • **Great Grooms**

Irish Bookcase

• ***1825***

An unusual Irish Regency mahogany carved library bookcase with good colour and patination. Formerly the property of Dr. John Shanley, one of the founders of the Irish Red Cross movement.

• *253cm x 180cm x 48cm*

• **£28,000** • **Freshfords**

Mahogany Bookcase

• ***1860***

English Victorian mahogany bookcase, crowned by a broken pediment. Features three glazed doors above, with a writing slope concealed behind sliding panels, and three panelled cupboards below.

• *190cm x 150cm*

• **£3,250** • **Old Cinema**

William IV Bookcase

• ***1830–37***

William IV open-top bookcase fitted with four shelves, and four panelled doors below.

• *170cm x 210cm*

• **£9,500** • **C.H. Major**

Victorian Bookcase

• ***circa 1890***

Victorian walnut bookcase with two glazed doors above, two drawers and cupboards below, made by Shootbird & Son. Complete with original fittings and keys.

• *150cm x 85cm*

• **£2,500** • **Old Cinema**

Expert Tips

When purchasing a bookcase, it is always good to remember to take your rule or tape measure with you to double-check that the item will fit the required space.

Boxes

Rosewood Tea Caddy ⌄

• ***late 19th century***
Simple, rosewood tea caddy comprising two compartments for different blends. Decorated with brass on the clasp and lid. This caddy incorporates a magnificent cut-glass sugar bowl.
• *width 25cm*
• £220 • **Ian Spencer**

Ivory Sewing Box ⌄

• ***circa 1830***
Magnificent early 19th-century vizagapatnum engraved and etched ivory sewing box with side drawer and sandalwood interior, in the form of a house with chimney finial and monogrammed cartouche.
• *height 14cm*
• £2,250 • **J. & T. Stone**

Penwork Tea Caddy ›

• ***circa 1825***
Exceptional, Regency penwork double tea caddy, decorated with chinoiserie scenes of a festive parade inside and out. The caddy has matching side handles, brass lion feet and a cut crystal sugar bowl.
• *height 18cm*
• £8,950
• **J. & T. Stone**

Hexagonal Tea Caddy ⌃

• ***circa 1785***
Late 18th-century, George III hexagonal, gilded, rolled-paper single tea caddy of unusual open design.
• *height 15cm*
• £2,450
• **J. & T. Stone**

Tortoiseshell Tea Caddy ⌃

• ***1830***
Very rare early 19th-century Regency pressed tortoiseshell two-compartment tea caddy, with ribbed and bowed front panels, domed top, silver stringing and insignia plate.
• *height 18cm*
• £8,950 • **J. & T. Stone**

Thoya Wood Tea Caddy ⌄

• ***1775***
George III, 18th-century thoya tea caddy of outstanding quality, heavily decorated with oval shell paterae with matched inner lid, burr walnut and satin wood banding.
• *height 14cm*
• £2,250 • **J. & T. Stone**

Victoria Wooden Dressing Case ⌄

• ***circa 1864***
Very unusual, Victorian, wooden dressing case with 11 extensively engraved silver-topped jars and containers marked 1864. Two secret drawers. Signed by W. H. Toole.
• £9,950
• **J. & T. Stone**

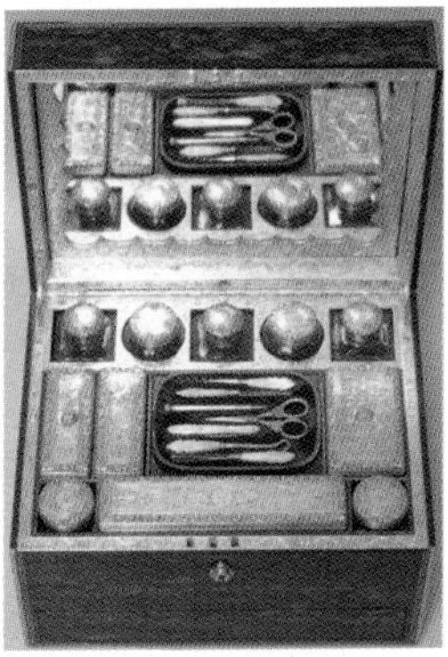

Expert Tips

Price is generally determined by quality and materials used, as well as age and rarity. In general, boxes made from wood or papier maché are widely available and most affordable.

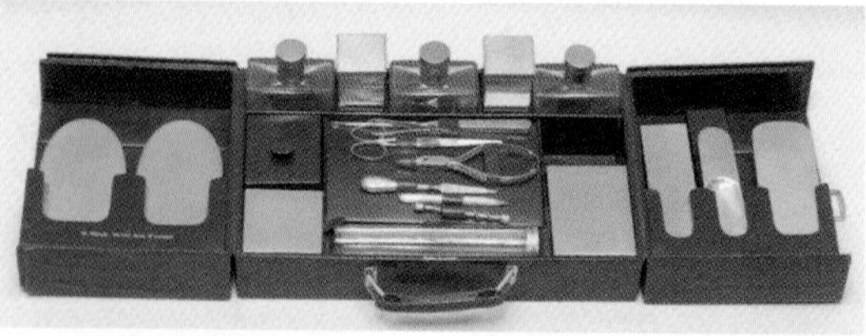

Travelling Dressing Case ◄

- ***circa* 1934**

An early 20th-century, fine-quality, Art Deco, crocodile-skin, gentleman's travelling dressing case. Made by Cartier of London. Hallmarked silver, inscribed "Sir W. Rollo".

- £3,995 • **J. & T. Stone**

Sewing Box ▲

- ***1832***

Exceptional, tortoiseshell sewing box with extensive mother-of-pearl floral inlay. With pull-out lower drawer and a note from the original owner.

- *height 14cm*
- £4,950 • **J. & T. Stone**

English Tortoiseshell Tea Caddy ▲

- ***circa* 1850**

Mid-19th-century English bow-front tortoiseshell tea caddy. Contains a mother-of-pearl floral inlay to the front panel. A fine quality piece.

- *height 33cm*
- £2,875
- **J. de Haan**

Expert Tips

Tunbridgeware originated around Tunbridge Wells 300 years ago and is a form of veneered decoration made entirely from the contrasting grains and colours of local woods. Tunbridgeware boxes are much in demand.

Russian Hatbox ▼

- ***circa* 1900**

An early 20th-century Russian hatbox made of birchwood, with a leather strap.

- *diameter 36.9cm*
- *height 22.5cm*
- £490 • **Rupert Cavendish**

Tortoiseshell and Silver Perfume Box ▼

- ***circa* 1918**

Original and complete. The box contains an inset of floral panel decorations. Made in England.

- *height 7.5cm*
- £1,270
- **Sue & Allan Thompson**

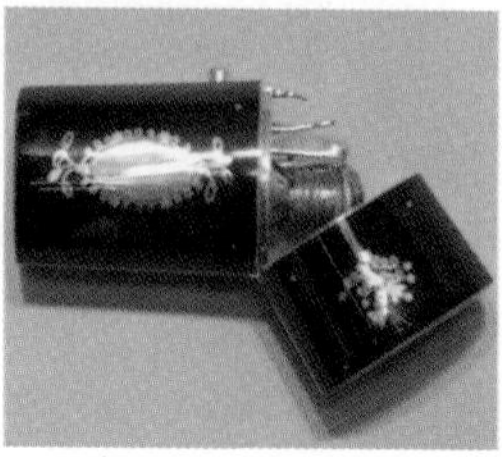

Gold Japanese Kogo ▲

- ***19th century***

Japanese, gold lacquered 19th-century kogo (box) in the form of a very unusual piebald puppy. The box is a container for incense.

- *height 6cm*
- £1,650 • **Gregg Baker**

Tunbridgeware Tea Caddy ▲

- ***circa* 1860**

Mid-19th-century, rectangular tea caddy. A view of Eridge Castle is shown on the lid. The box is made from rosewood with a keyhole in the panel of the box.

- *height 12cm*
- £625
- **J. de Haan**

Coromandel Dressing Box

- *circa 1857*

Coromandel dressing box with hall-marked, heavily chased, silver topped, cut glass bottles.

- *width 36cm*
- £3,500 • **Hygra**

Tortoiseshell Box

- *1930*

Atractive petite Art Deco tortoiseshell box.

- *length 10cm*
- £145 • **Abacus Antiques**

Wig Box

- *late 18th century*

Lacquered wig box with painted floral decoration.

- *length 30cm*
- £950 • **O.F. Wilson**

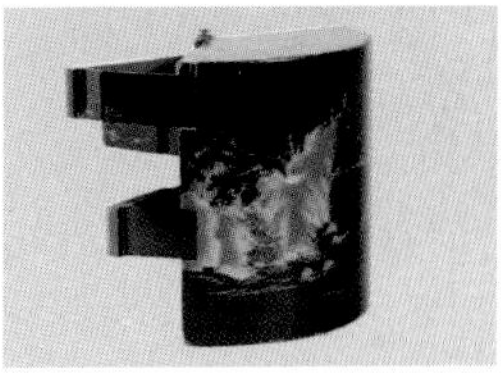

Japanese Lacquer Box

- *circa 1870*

A Japanese lacquer, fan-shaped and inspired box with multi-layered drawers and raised gold decoration.

- *height 20cm*
- £330 • **Hygra**

Chinese Dressing Chest

- *early 19th century*

A Chinese hardwood dressing chest with double-hinged, mirror-lined top profusely decorated with mother-of-pearl.

- *width 27cm*
- £950 • **Hygra**

Regency Tea Caddy

- *1820*

Regency tortoiseshell, double tea caddy with pagoda top, ivory facing, silver stringing, initial plate and escutcheon.

- *15cm x 18cm x 12cm*
- £3,950 • **J. & T. Stone**

Cribbage Box

- *circa 1790*

Fine Anglo-Indian vizagapatnum incised ivory cribbage box.

- *width 18cm*
- £1,600 • **Hygra**

Knife Box

- *circa 1770*

A George III flame mahogany knife box with satinwood inlay and brass fittings.

- *37cm x 21.7cm*
- £995 • Great Grooms

Georgian Tea Caddy

- *circa 1810*

A Georgian burr yew tea caddy with two compartments, standing on scrolled brass feet.

- *22cm x 30cm*
- £450 • Barham

Chinese Lacquer Box

- *1830*

Chinese lacquer octagonal box with gilded chinoiserie and floral designs, on gilded claw feet.

- *15cm x 34cm x 23cm*
- £1,850 • O.F. Wilson

Pillow Box

- *circa 1880*

Chinese pillow box made from wood with brass handles and escutcheon plate. The lid is shaped as the pillow.

- *14cm x 31cm*
- £150 • Great Grooms

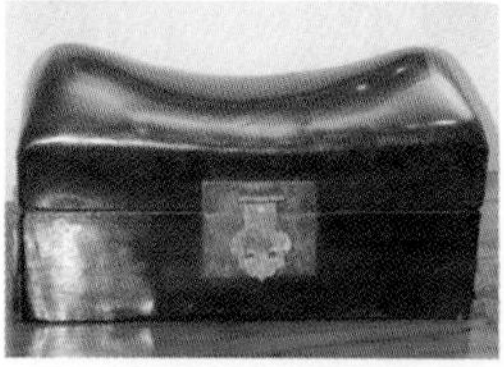

Korean Lacquer Box

- *17th–18th century*

Lacquer box and cover of oval form, set with a single European engraved floral design hinge and a later European lock plate. The cover and sides decorated with a free scrolling design of flowers and leaves inlaid in mother of pearl, the stem of the vine inlaid in flat silvered wire, all on a black lacquer ground.

- *9.2cm x 37.5cm*
- £6,500 • Gerard Hawthorn

Indian Dowry Box

- *19th century*

A copper dowry box from the Rajasthan province, with geometric enamelled designs, standing on shaped feet.

- *39cm x 28cm*
- £295 • Gordon Reece

Chinese Ivory Casket

- *18th–19th century*

A fine Canton ivory casket fitted with European carrying handle, lock plate, corner reinforcement and ball and claw feet. The red silk-lined interior is fitted with three Chinese pewter-lined ivory caddies, the pierced ivory panelling of the caddies is decorated with geometric diapers and floral designs within ruyi-head borders. The casket is decorated with low relief panels of landscapes and flowers.

- *13.6cm x 26cm*
- £8,500 • Gerard Hawthorn

Miniature Postbox

- *1900*

Late Victorian oak miniature postbox with original inset rate card, brass plate inscribed "Letters", and carved leaf top.

- *height 38cm*
- £2,950 • J. & T. Stone

Small Lacquer Chest

- *late 18th century*

A Chinese small lacquer chest with three tiers of drawers behind two doors painted with extensive chinoiserie designs.

- *height 24cm*
- £2,250 • O.F. Wilson

Chinese Tea Caddy

- *circa 1840*

Shaped and lacquered Chinese tea caddy with gold decoration, on carved dragon feet.

- *width 21cm*
- £850 • Hygra

French Domed Box

- *19th century*

Box with domed lid decorated with faux tortoiseshell design.

- *length 30cm*
- £950 • O.F. Wilson

Oblong Tea Caddy

- *circa 1770*

Fine eighteenth-century tea caddy of oblong form in native and imported hardwoods, with mother-of-pearl accents, having a brass handle and paw feet.

- *width 22cm*
- £950 • Hygra

Amboyna Tea Caddy

- *circa 1830*

A George IV amboyna tea caddy of sarcophagus form with side handles, mother-of-pearl roundels, pewter stringing, and an interior with twin compartments.

- *length 30cm*
- £1,200 • O.F. Wilson

Games Compendium

- *1880*

Late Victorian dome-topped and front-opening coromandel wood games compendium with a comprehensive assortment of games including chess, dominoes, backgammon, tiddlywinks and numerous set of playing cards and counters all housed in a front compartment and two lift-out trays.

- *18cm x 33.5cm x 23cm*
- £4,950 • J. & T. Stone

Chinese Canton Enamel Panelled Box

- *18th century*

A fine Canton enamel-panelled huanghuali box and cover of rectangular form and regular construction with floating panels, mitred corners and hidden dovetails, set with two bail handles at the sides and a wood lock plate.

- *18.1cm x 31.7cm*
- £6,000 • Gerard Hawthorn

Bureaux

Pine Secretaire
- ***20th century***

A painted pine miniature secretaire with broken pediment above the fall, fitted interior, and shaped bracket feet.
- *height 80cm*
- £675 • **Solaris**

William IV Secretaire
- ***1835***

An William IV flame mahogany secretaire chiffonier with fall front and heavy scrolling to the sides of the panelled cupboards.
- *145cm x 94cm x 50cm*
- £1,750 • **Tredantiques**

Mahogany Bureau
- ***1740***

Mahogany bureau with well-fitted walnut interior, various pigeon holes and hidden drawers, brass ring handles and escutcheons, on moulded bracket feet.
- *92cm x 109cm*
- £6,500 • **Pimlico Antiques**

Walnut Bureau
- ***circa 1810***

George III walnut bureau with cross banding, the fall enclosing a well-fitted interior, with four graduated drawers with original brass fittings on moulded bracket feet.
- *99cm x 70cm*
- £4,500 • **Sign of the Times**

Empire Bureau Commode
- ***circa 1820***

Swedish mahogany Empire bureau commode with fitted interior and fold down flap above three deep drawers, flanked by turned columns with gilt mounts.
- *94cm x 111cm x 51cm*
- £6,500 • **R. Cavendish**

French Empire Secretaire
- ***circa 1800s***

A mahogany French Empire *secretaire abattant* with a marble top, turned columns and pierced ormolu mounts.
- *height 140cm x 80cm*
- £5,500 • **C.H. Major**

Mahogany Bureau

- ***circa 1780***

An 18th-century mahogany bureau without leather inlay.

- *height 1.02m*
- £3,800 • Mora & Upham

George III Bureau

- ***early 19th century***

Mahogany inlaid bureau with fitted interior shaped upon slightly splayed feet.

- *height 1.45m*
- £2,200 • Old Cinema

Roll-Top Bureau

- ***circa 1880***

Burr walnut with serpentine front, fitted interior and three drawers. Standing on scrolled feet.

- *height 2.26m*
- £8,250 • Antique Warehouse

Campaign Chest

- ***circa 1840***

English mahogany secretaire campaign chest with pull-out flap, fitted compartments and brass mounts.

- *height 1.10m*
- £4,200 • Riverbank

Expert Tips

The earliest bureaux were made in two parts, a bureau on top and a chest base below, each with its own carrying handles. Ones to look out for are transitional examples, made in one piece but still with the accoutrements of two.

Cylinder Bureau

- ***circa 1800***

A fine early 19th-century George III mahogany cylinder bureau on original castors.

- *height 1.41m*
- £10,500 • Westland & Co

Military Chest

- ***19th century***

Campaign/military chest in camphor wood with brass handles.

- *height 1.06m*
- £3,500 • Tower Bridge

Cylinder Bureau ➤

• *circa 1890*
Mahogany bureau with boxwood and satinwood crossbanding.
• *height 1.12m*
• £7,000 • **Judy Fox**

Oak Bureau ▲

• *circa 1750*
Shaped interior with drawers and pigeon holes, on bracket feet.
• *height 1.35m*
• £2,450 • **M.J. Bowdery**

English Country Bureau ▲

• *18th century*
Crossbanded in mahogany with swan brass handles and shell inlay.
• *height 1.02m*
• £3,575 • **I.& J.L. Brown**

Georgian Bureau ▲

• *circa 1810*
Mahogany bureau with green leather inset and fitted interior.
• *height 1.06m*
• £1,400 • **Zai Davar**

Expert Tips

All other elements being equal, the smaller the bureau the more valuable it is likely to be.

Fall Front Bureau ◄

• *circa 1735*
George II red walnut bureau with well fitted breakfront interior.
• *height 1.03m*
• £5,750 • **J. Collins**

Satinwood Roll-Top Bureau

• *1890*
An early nineteenth century-style bureau in satinwood. The gallery comprises three drawers above the roll-top desk and three drawers below, standing on square tapered legs.
• *100cm x 90cm x 48cm*
• £6,000 • J. Fox

Two-Drawer Secretaire

• *1830*
Secretaire in pale walnut fitted with drawer in the frieze and two drawers below the fall.
• *146cm x 96cm x 40cm*
• £4,600 • O.F. Wilson

Mahogany Secretaire

• *circa 1820*
Mahogany secretaire with ormolu mounts, the fall with fitted interior above two moulded cupboard doors raised on splayed bracket feet.
• *height 140cm*
• £3,500 • N. E. McAuliffe

Expert Tips

As a general rule the smaller a desk or bookcase the more valuable it is, but look out for shortened bookcases. It was a common practice to cut down these pieces so that they would fit smaller rooms.

Bureau Bookcase

• *1850*
Victorian figured walnut roll-top bureau with fitted interior below glazed doors with bookshelves.
• *231cm x 105cm x 60cm*
• £9,500 • J. Fox

Gustavian Secretaire

• *circa 1800*
A painted Louis XVI Swedish Gustavian secretaire, with moulded ogée cornice above two cupboard doors and pull-down writing flap with four tiers of drawers below, on bracket feet.
• *190cm x 99cm x 51cm*
• £3,400 • R. Cavendish

Cabinets

Oriental Cabinet

• ***19th century***
A lacquered cabinet on a stand with a well-fitted interior of ten compartments.
• *height 1.36m*
• **£2,600** • **Ranby Hall**

Continental Vitrine

• ***circa 1830***
A walnut-panelled vitrine with gilt mounts and lyre feet.
• *height 1.6m*
• **£1,350** • **Travers**

Side Cabinet

• ***circa 1860***
A Victorian, walnut-veneered serpentine side cabinet.
• *height 1.08m*
• **£1,980** • **Ranby Hall**

Mahogany Side Cabinet

• ***circa 1790***
A cabinet of the Sheraton period, of crossbanded satinwood with ebony and boxwood stringing.
• *height 89.5cm*
• **£8,500** • **J. Collins**

Pier Cabinet

• ***circa 1865***
A Victorian ebonised two-door pier cabinet inlaid with amboyna.
• *height 1.06m*
• **£2,600** • **Judy Fox**

Walnut Pier Cabinet

• ***circa 1860***
Cabinet with a mirror-fronted door panel and gilt-metal mounts.
• *height 1.08m*
• **£1,980**
• **Ranby Hall**

Lacquered Cabinet

• ***circa 1770***
A good, small English table-top cabinet with chinoiserie scenes.
• *height 69cm*
• **£3,800** • **P. L. James**

Collector's Cabinet

- *circa 1900*

Steel and glass collector's cabinet with brass mountings.

- *height 1.25m*
- £1,500 • David Ford

Bedside Cupboard

- *circa 1820*

A mahogany French Empire cupboard with ormolu and gilt mountings and a marble top.

- *height 77cm*
- £1,950 • O. F. Wilson

Chinese Herbal Cabinet

- *19th century*

A red lacquered herbalist's cabinet with Chinese characters.

- *height 2.12m*
- £1,850 • Riverbank

Hanging Corner Cabinet

- *circa 1740*

The cabinet has two double panelled doors with starburst marquetry inlay designs.

- *height 1.14m*
- £1,575 • Red Lion

George II Pot Cupboards

- *circa 1750*

A pair of burr-walnut pot cabinets.

- *height 70cm*
- £1,675 • C. Preston

Continental Cabinet

- *circa 1800*

Unusual mahogany cabinet with a shaped panel door and moulded square taper legs.

- *height 1.54m*
- £1,495 • M. J. Bowdery

Breakfront Cabinet

- *1866*

A mahogany cabinet by Gillow, signed Thos Whiteside. With architectural and leaf decoration.

- *height 98cm*
- £6,850
- Chambers

Mahogany Side Cabinets ⌄

- *circa 1880*

Matched pair of mahogany side cabinets with marble tops.

- *height 84cm*
- £1,150 • Ranby Hall

Corner Cabinet ›

- *circa 1910*

One of a pair of Edwardian mahogany cabinets with glazed upper part and a cupboard base.

- *height 2.16m*
- £750 • Canonbury

Oak Corner Cabinet ^

- *circa 1780*

A full standing cupboard with patina and original mounts.

- *height 2.09m*
- £3,975 • Red Lion

Italian Walnut Cabinet ^

- *circa 1880*

A cabinet in the Bambocci manner, decorated with figural uprights and panelled doors.

- *height 91.5cm*
- £2,400 • Westland & Co

French Pearwood Cabinet ⌄

- *circa 1830*

Carved pearwood cabinet from Normandy. Good colour with diamond-shaped panels and chamfered columns on both sides.

- *height 1.23m*
- £2,750 • Town & Country

Corner Cupboard ⌄

- *circa 1780*

A rare George III, chinoiserie-patterned, Japanned, standing corner cupboard.

- *height 2.03m*
- £40,000 • Norman Adams

Secretaire/Cabinet ⌄

- *19th century*

A boulle-work ebonised secretaire with rosewood interior and various compartments.

- *height 1.36m*
- £2,750 • Ranby Hall

Empire-Style Cabinets

• *1880*
One of a pair of Empire-style satinwood side cabinets, the central panelled cupboard with a lyre-shaped ormolu mount, on tapered legs.
• *75cm x 42cm x 40cm*
• £1,385 • Ranby Hall

Lacquered Corner Cabinet

• *1750*
A George III black lacquered corner cabinet, decorated with a chinoiserie-style relief.
• *58cm x 90cm x 38cm*
• £2,950 • Mac Humble

Victorian Credenza

• *circa 1860*
A Victorian ebonised credenza with oval painted porcelain panels with gilt mounts and banding .
• *110cm x 178cm x 37cm*
• £3,250 • Ranby Hall

Japanese Cabinet

• *Edo period*
A mizuya dansu, or cabinet, from the late Edo period in cryptomeria. The drawer fronts in zelkova.
• *175cm x 170cm*
• £7,000 • Gordon Reece

Tibetan Chest

• *circa 1890*
A Tibetan chest with carved and painted decoration depicting long life symbols.
• *94cm x 107cm*
• £2,300 • Great Grooms

Biedermeier Cabinet

• *1920*
A Biedermeier light mahogany cabinet inlaid with figurative and floral designs.
• *height 130cm*
• £3,850 • Ranby Hall

Medicine Cabinet

• *circa 1890*
Stripped and polished nickel-plated bathroom cabinet.
• *45cm x 30cm x 15cm*
• £245 • After Noah (KR)

Corner Cupboard

- ***18th century***

An oak corner cupboard with cavetto flat top.

- *105cm x 85cm*
- £1,045 • **Great Grooms**

Cross-Banded Cupboard

- ***circa 1775***

An early George III oak and mahogany cross-banded hanging oak cupboard.

- *42 cm x 76cm x 98 cm*
- £2,450 • **Great Grooms**

Display Cabinet

- ***18th century***

An eighteenth-century Dutch inlaid walnut display cabinet with moulded doors.

- *77cm x 82cm x 27cm*
- £4,450 • **Paul Hopwell**

Expert Tips

Highly decorative display cabinets that contain porcelain plaques must be completely intact and uncracked. The break front cabinet or credenza is highly desirable and it is important to remember that, in the case of ebonised cabinets, the value can be reduced.

Breakfront Victorian Credenza

- ***1860***

A breakfront Victorian credenza, with amboyna wood, original painted porcelain plaques and gilt bronze mounts.

- *109cm x 186cm x 45cm*
- £12,000 • **J. Fox**

Georgian Bow-Fronted Cupboard

- ***circa 1810***

A Georgian glazed bow-front corner cupboard with gothic-style glazing bars.

- *100cm x 53cm*
- £1,200 • **Tredantiques**

Regency Mahogany Side Cabinet

- ***circa 1800***

A Regency flame-mahogany side cabinet with oval satinwood inlay door panels, banded in satinwood. Raised on splayed bracket feet.

- *105cm x 97cm x 40cm*
- £1,650 • **Ranby Hall**

French Gothic Cabinet

- *1910*

A French gothic carved oak cocktail cabinet in seventeenth century-style with extensive gothic tracery.

- *182cm x 112cm x 58cm*
- £2,250 • Tredantiques

Corner Cabinet

- *1890*

An English oak corner cabinet with glazed door, ogee moulding, with pierced carved frieze below, on three square straight legs.

- *185cm x 103cm x 70cm*
- £1,350 • Tredantiques

Painted Sideboard

- ***circa* 1800**

A painted Louis XVI Swedish Gustavian sideboard with moulded geometric designs.

- *98cm x 107cm x 51cm*
- £4,500 • R. Cavendish

Toy Cupboard

- *1900s*

A pine cupboard with two panel doors below a moulded pediment with original brass fittings.

- *142cm x 137cm x 56cm*
- £420 • Old School

School Cupboard

- *1900s*

English oak school cupboard with two interior shelves and moulded panel doors with bun handles.

- *140cm x 153cm*
- £600 • Old School

Ebonised Cabinet

- *19th century*

A fine German nineteenth-century ebonised cabinet with detailed Dresden porcelain plaques and figures.

- *180cm x 130cm x 52cm*
- £55,000 • Sinai Antiques

Oak Corner Cupboard

- *18th century*

An oak corner cupboard with moulded dentil course.

- *98cm x 94cm*
- £1,095 • Great Grooms

Canterburies

Music Stand

• *circa 1920*
Regency-style painted, wrought-iron music canterbury with profuse floral pierced decoration and splayed legs.
• *height 68cm*
• £1,275 • **Browns**

Victorian Canterbury

• *circa 1875*
Burr walnut Victorian canterbury with ornate pierced gallery top and pierced divisions, the whole raised on turned feet.
• *height 87cm*
• £1,495 • **Fulham**

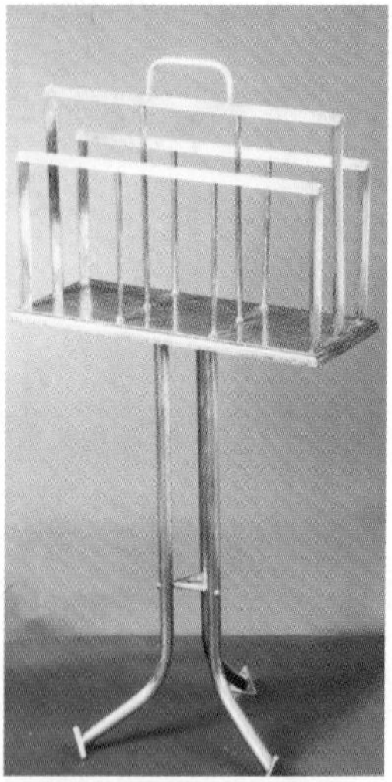

Brass Magazine Rack

• *circa 1915*
An Edwardian brass magazine rack, with carrying handle.
• *height 80cm*
• £245 • **Castlegate**

Victorian Canterbury

• *circa 1850*
Burr walnut with turned supports on original porcelain castors.
• *height 55cm*
• £1,400 • **Judy Fox**

Victorian Canterbury

• *circa 1880*
Mahogany wood with turned supports and legs and one drawer.
• *height 56cm*
• £1,025 • **Antiques**

Mahogany Canterbury

• *circa 1815*
A fine-quality English mahogany canterbury with turned columns and legs with brass castors.
• *height 54cm*
• £2,800 • **Tredantiques**

Expert Tips

The legs of canterburies are particularly vulnerable. Check them for evidence of repair or replacement.

Three-Compartment Canterbury ➤

- *1880*

A Victorian walnut canterbury with three compartments and drawer to front. With pierced frieze to the sides and turned legs on brass castors.

- *44cm x 59cm x 38cm*
- £1,250 • J. Fox

Victorian Canterbury with Writing Slide ➤

- *1880*

A Victorian walnut canterbury with writing slide and drawer on the base, with turned bun feet.

- *79cm x 61cm x 48cm*
- £2,500 • J. Fox

Sheraton Canterbury ➤

- *1860*

A Sheraton mahogany, four-division canterbury with a half shaped carrying handle, removable division slides, and a single drawer to the base, with turned legs on brass castors.

- *66cm x 49cm x 43cm*
- £4,850 • M.W. & H.L.

George III Canterbury ➤

- *1810*

George III mahogany canterbury with single drawer, standing on turned baluster feet on brass castors.

- *height 65cm*
- £2,850 • Mac Humble

Regency Canterbury ➤

- *1820–30*

Regency rosewood canterbury with three compartments and single drawer standing on four turned legs with original castors.

- *48cm x 48cm x 38cm*
- £1,695 • Old Cinema

Chairs

Tapestry Armchair

• ***circa* 1680**
A rare French hardwood armchair with tapestry cover.
• *height 1.21m*
• **£6,500 • Raffety & Walwyn**

Grotto Harp Stool

• ***circa* 1850**
A grotto stool with scallop shell seat on acanthus cabriole legs and claw feet. The whole in gilt.
• *height 65cm*
• **£1,600 • Lynda Franklin**

Regency Bergère

• ***circa* 1810**
A very good, large Regency bergère chair.
• *height 96cm*
• **£6,200 • Christopher Preston**

Biedermeier-Style Chair

• ***circa* 1915**
A pair of Swedish masur birch chairs in cream ultra-suede.
• *height 93cm*
• **£4,900 • Rupert Cavendish**

Sheraton Chair

• ***circa* 1780**
An English green-painted chair decorated with floral designs.
• *height 90cm*
• **£4,600 • O.F. Wilson**

Bamboo Chair

• ***circa* 1830**
A Regency single chair painted to simulate bamboo.
• *height 87cm*
• **£175 • O.F. Wilson**

Hall Chair

• ***circa* 1850**
An English mahogany mid-19th-century hall chair, with scrolled arms and an extensively turned frame, the whole resting on bun feet. The chair is in perfect condition, and reupholstered, with a red and gold Gothic pattern.
• *height 98cm*
• **£1,800 • Gabrielle de Giles**

Writing Chair ▲

• *circa 1840*

A fine 19th-century Portuguese carved rosewood writing chair.

• *height 98cm*

• £20,000 • **Norman Adams**

Provincial Fauteuil ▲

• *circa 1820*

An oversized French provincial walnut open armchair, covered in moleskin, with escargot feet.

• *width 1.15m*

• £1,950 • **French Country**

Red Walnut Chairs ▼

• *circa 1730*

A fine pair of red walnut chairs with cabriole legs.

• *height 96cm*

• £9,500 • **Raffety & Walwyn**

Victorian Chairs ▼

• *circa 1885*

Set of four rosewood chairs with cabriole legs and pierced leaf decoration.

• *height 85cm*

• £950 • **Castlegate**

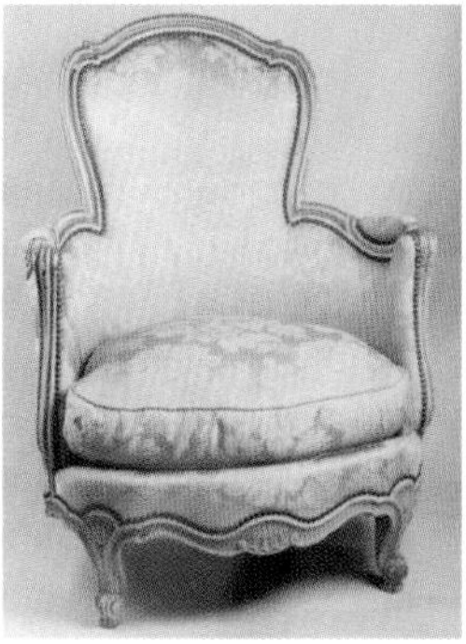

French Bergères ◄

• *19th century*

A pair of French bergères painted with scroll and shell motifs on scrolled feet.

• *height 1.03m*

• £2,550 • **Lynda Franklin**

Bedroom Chair ▲

• *circa 1880*

A French gold bedroom chair with original upholstery.

• *height 90cm*

• £190 • **Lacquer Chest**

Piano Chair ▲

• *circa 1860*

A mahogany balloon back revolving piano chair.

• *height 80cm*

• £550 • **North West 8**

Expert Tips

Beware overstuffed drop-in seats. If these have been pushed hard onto the frame, they may have put pressure on the rail joints, causing them to split.

George II Chairs

• *circa 1740*
Set of four oak chairs with spoon backrest and cabriole front legs.
• *height 98cm*
• £950 • Albany

Ladder-Back Chair

• *circa 1730*
A single elm chair with turned legs and nipple decoration.
• *height 97cm*
• £125 • Castlegate

Hepplewhite Chairs

• *circa 1780*
A set of eight mahogany shield-back dining chairs.
• *height 92.5cm*
• £60,000 • Norman Adams

Set of Chairs

• *circa 1900*
A set of four painted and gilded Northern Italian chairs with shell and mushroom motifs, on cabriole legs.
• *height 85cm*
• £1,450 • Andrew Bewick

French Fauteuil

• *circa 1770*
With terracotta highlights, light blue cloth and floral designs.
• *height 91cm*
• £2,200 • O.F. Wilson

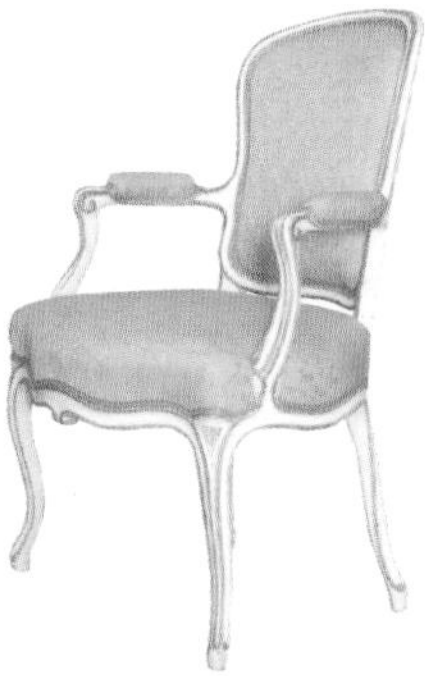

Bergère Library Armchair

• *circa 1830*
Mahogany with turned legs and wickerwork back and sides.
• *height 91cm*
• £990 • Castlegate

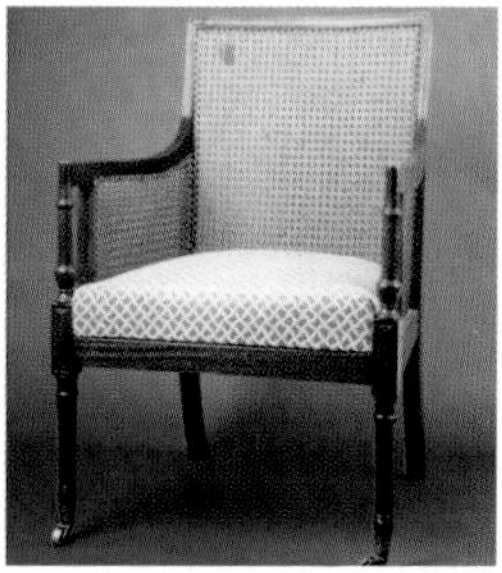

Egyptian Design Chair

• *circa 1920*
Pair of English elbow chairs with hand-worked tapestry covers.
• *height 94cm*
• £4,950
• M. Wakelin & H. Linfield

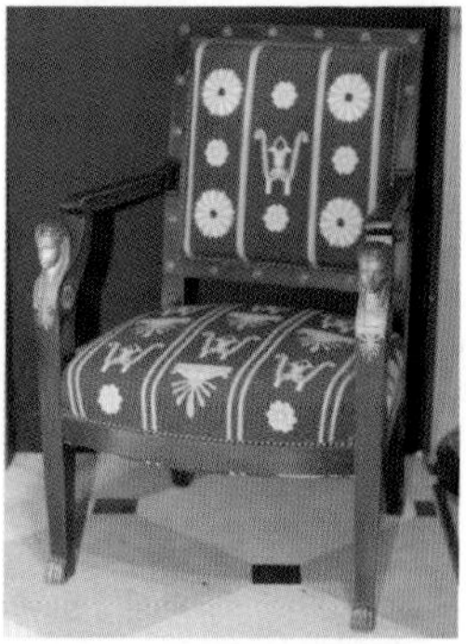

Mahogany Chairs

- *circa 1755*

Set of six chairs with caned seats, pierced back and sabre back-legs.

- *height 82cm*
- £3,750 • **Lesley Bragge**

Expert Tips

The more chairs in a set, the greater the value. Thus a pair will be worth more than twice the value of a single chair, but a set of eight will be worth perhaps 20 times the value of a single chair. The most valuable sets will include one or two carvers.

Child's Rocking chair

- *circa 1790*

An 18th-century turned ash and elm child's rocking chair.

- *height 51cm*
- £265 • **Castlegate**

Country Dining Chairs

- *circa 1885*

Set of four Arts and Crafts elm chairs with tapered legs.

- *height 90cm*
- £550 • **Castlegate**

Winged Armchair

- *circa 1880*

An armchair raised on ebonised cabriole legs with pad feet.

- *height 1.3m*
- £1,850 • **Ranby Hall**

Empire-Style Chair

- *circa 1900*

Pair of Swedish, mahogany chairs with sabre back legs and gilded decoration to the backrest.

- *height 84cm*
- £2,300 • **Rupert Cavendish**

Lacquered Chair

- *19th century*

By Hitchcock, Connecticut. With fruit and leaf decoration.

- *height 83cm*
- £1,400 • **Lynda Franklin**

American Rocker

- *circa 1880*

With profuse turned decoration and tartan upholstery.

- *height 1.03m*
- £395 • **Castlegate**

Hepplewhite-Period Chair

• *circa 1780*
In mahogany with pierced backrest and turned legs.
• *height 88cm*
• £520 • **Castlegate**

French Fauteuils

• *circa 1755*
A pair of open-arm gilt wood chairs, stamped "Iocob".
• *height 88cm*
• £5,500 • **Michael Davidson**

Set of Dining Chairs

• *circa 1780*
A set of six 18th-century fruitwood dining chairs, set on turned, candlestick legs, with classical motifs throughout.
• £3,200 • **Sieff**

Neo-Gothic Armchair

• *19th century*
Impressively carved chair, with Gothic tracery, twisted and fluted decoration and solid wood seat, the whole on turned legs.
• *height 1.31m*
• £1,750 • **The Old Cinema**

Library Chair

• *circa 1810*
A deep button-backed library chair with original upholstery.
• *height 1.06m*
• £2,200 • **Riverbank**

Leather Desk Chair

• *circa 1885*
Leather and mahogany chair with brass stud work, on tapered legs.
• *height 99cm*
• £260 • **Youlls**

Mahogany Dining Chairs

• *19th century*
Six chairs with moulded camel back and good patination.
• *height 96.5cm*
• £7,500 • **J. Collins**

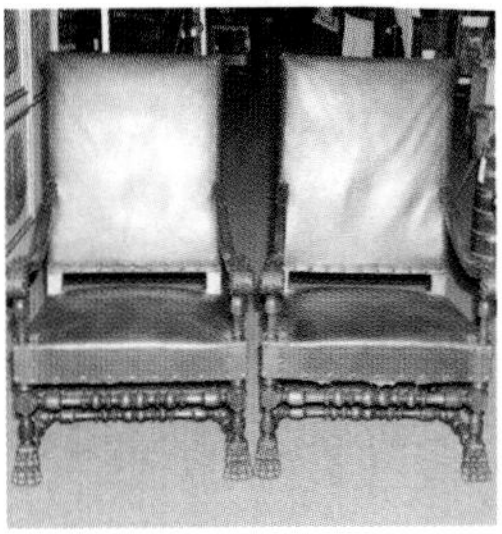

Walnut Armchairs

- *circa 1880*

A pair of finely carved French walnut armchairs with original leather upholstery and profusely turned stretchers. The chairs are carved with leaf patterns adorning the bottom and tops of the arms. The legs terminate in lion-paw feet.

- *height 94cm*
- £3,200 • **Tredantiques**

Expert Tips

Beware of "scrambling", where unscrupulous dealers – or innocent householders – add to a set of chairs by taking some of them apart and replacing parts with new members, making up new chairs from old parts.

French Walnut Chairs

- *19th century*

A pair of walnut chairs with carved leaf decoration and scrolling designs, on cabriole legs.

- *height 83cm*
- £1,450 • **Lynda Franklin**

Gilt Armchairs

- *circa 1880*

A pair of French armchairs with carved detail on frame and arms.

- *height 1.03m*
- £2,500 • **Canonbury**

Child's Highchair

- *circa 1800*

A bergère highchair with turned front and splayed rear legs. Easily converted to a table and chair, with a central screw to table base.

- *height 94cm*
- £1,350 • **John Clay**

Victorian Sofa Chairs

- *19th century*

A pair of Victorian sofa chairs.

- *height 40cm*
- £1,650 • **Fiona McDonald**

Windsor Chair

- *circa 1760*

Windsor chair in ash and elm with comb back and cabriole legs.

- *height 1.08m*
- £5,800 • **Raffety & Walwyn**

Sheraton Armchair

- *circa 1795*

A Sheraton-period painted and gilded armchair.

- *height 88.5cm*
- £8,000 • **Norman Adams**

Windsor Side Chairs

• *circa 1810*
A pair of comb-back Windsor side chairs with turned legs.
• *height 87cm*
• **£145** • **Castlegate**

Invalid's Chair

• *circa 1910*
An invalid's chair with original green upholstery.
• *height 1.36m*
• **£190** • **Lacquer Chest**

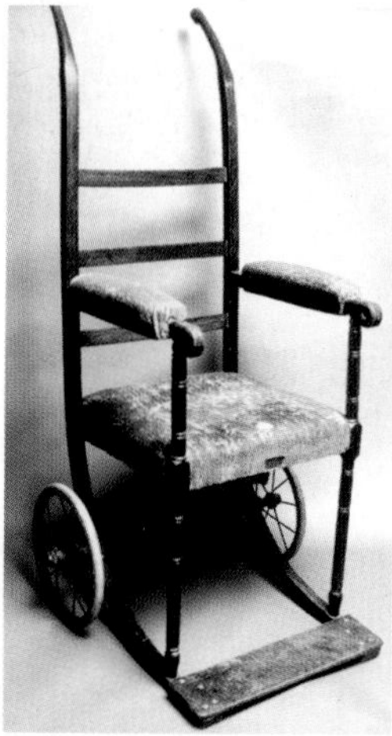

George I Oak Chairs

• *circa 1720*
A solid pair of George I oak chairs with good colour.
• *height 99cm*
• **£595** • **Red Lion**

Louis XVI Bergère

• ***19th century***
A Louis XVI-style bergère with gold leaf on tapered, reeded legs.
• *height 1.06m*
• **£1,395** • **Red Lion**

Simulated Bamboo Chairs

• *circa 1820*
Set of six Regency simulated and painted bamboo chairs.
• *height 84cm*
• **£1,200** • **North West 8**

French Dining Chairs

• *circa 1885*
A set of eight French Empire-style dining chairs.
• *height 91cm*
• **£4,500** • **North West 8**

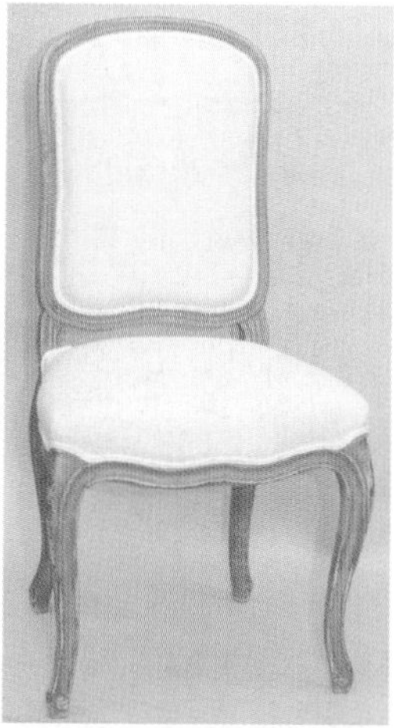

Expert Tips

Large sets of chairs have often been broken up and carvers manufactured from them. Check the wood match on the arms of the carver and, particularly, the size of the seat. The carver should be at least two inches wider than the other chairs.

Mahogany Hall Chair

• *circa 1820*
English Regency period, of unusual shape, with sabre legs.
• *height 80cm*
• **£4,650** • **O.F. Wilson**

Mahogany Child's Chair

• *1900*
Victorian mahogany child's chair with cane seat and back rest by J. & J. Cone.
• *66cm x 36cm*
• £230 • **John Clay**

Expert Tips

Always check for bad repairs as they can seriously affect a chair's strength and usability. Complete sets of 12 or more chairs are rare and expensive, even the quite late examples.

Swedish High-Sided Armchairs

• ***18th century***
A pair of Swedish armchairs with high back and sides with original velvet and tapestry.
• *height 95cm*
• £3,200 • **Solaris**

Library Chair

• ***early 19th century***
A leather button-backed library chair with lyre-shaped arms and carved decoration on turned feet.
• *114cm x 74cm*
• £1,400 • **John Clay**

Officer's Chair

• ***1901–10***
Edwardian Officer's revolving ladder back chair on brass castors.
• *88cm x 53cm*
• £665 • **Old Cinema**

Louis XV Chair

• ***1770***
Louis XV-period fauteuil painted white with moulded decoration and shaped apron on cabriole legs.
• *height 85cm*
• £2,200 • **O.F. Wilson**

Painted Fauteuils

• ***1780***
One of four painted Louis XVI French fauteuils with scrolled back and straight arms on turned legs.
• *86cm x 60cm x 47cm*
• £9,000 • **O.F. Wilson**

William IV Dining Chairs ➤

- *1830*

Set of six William IV mahogany dining chairs with curved backs. Re-upholstered with horsehair covers on turned legs.

- *52cm x 49cm x 55cm*
- £3,995 • **Old Cinema**

Child's Armchair ▲

- *circa 1830*

Nineteenth century ash and elm Windsor child's armchair.

- *92cm x 48cm x 42cm*
- £795 • **Rod Wilson**

Walnut Corner Chair ▲

- *1740*

A walnut corner chair with shaped backrest and carved apron, standing on pad feet.

- *125cm x 76cm x 65cm*
- £1,400 • **Midwinter**

Expert Tips

If a cushioned seat or stuffed back is still in possession of its original fabric or covering this can greatly enhance its value.

Italian Carver Chairs ◀

- *circa 1820*

A spectacular pair of Italian walnut carver chairs with ornately carved mythological dog heads to arms and back, heavy leaf decoration to legs, with paw feet. The seat and back upholstered with embossed leather.

- *153cm x 81cm x 61cm*
- £22,000 • **Simon Hatchwell**

Bergère Chair ▼

- *1840*

Mahogany bergère chair stamped "Windsor Castle, V.R."

- *92cm x 52cm*
- £6,500 • **Pimlico Antiques**

Ladder Back Chair ▲

- *1850*

A Lancashire elmwood ladder back chair with an unusually high back, rush seating, and turned legs.

- *123cm x 56cm x 42cm*
- £395 • **Lacquer Chest**

Spindle-Back Nursing Chair

- *circa 1820*

Lancashire spindle-back nursing chair, with rush seat on turned legs.

- *134cm x 54cm x 54cm*
- £295 • Rod Wilson

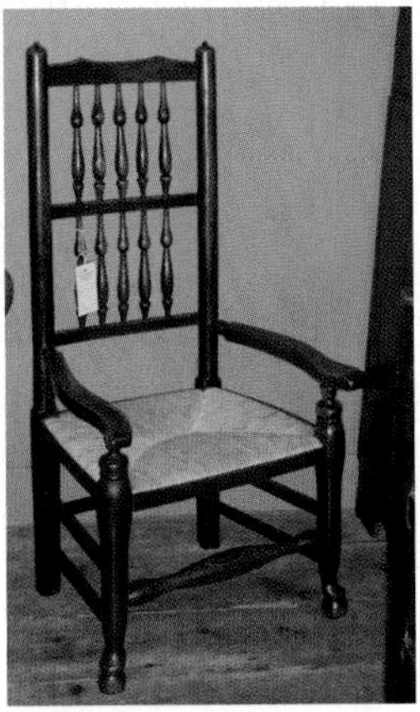

Oak Corner Chair

- *circa 1750*

Oak corner chair in the Chippendale style.

- *124cm x 70cm*
- £1,250 • Rod Wilson

Expert Tips

You need to maintain the patina of a chair by regular waxing with a good quality beeswax that is non-staining. Constant polishing with a stained wax will darken the patina and compromise the attraction of the furniture.

Regency Dining Chairs

- *1820*

A set of six regency chairs and two carvers, with curved backs and sabre legs.

- *height 81cm*
- £12,500 • C.H. Major

Queen Anne Chair

- *circa 1700*

Queen Anne oak transitional chair with good colour and patination.

- *146cm x 60cm x 51cm*
- £3,450 • Rod Wilson

Oak Country Chairs

- *1840*

One of four oak country chairs, with carved top rail, pierced splayed splat, and solid seat, on square moulded legs.

- *94cm x 48cm x 41cm*
- £1,800 • Lacquer Chest

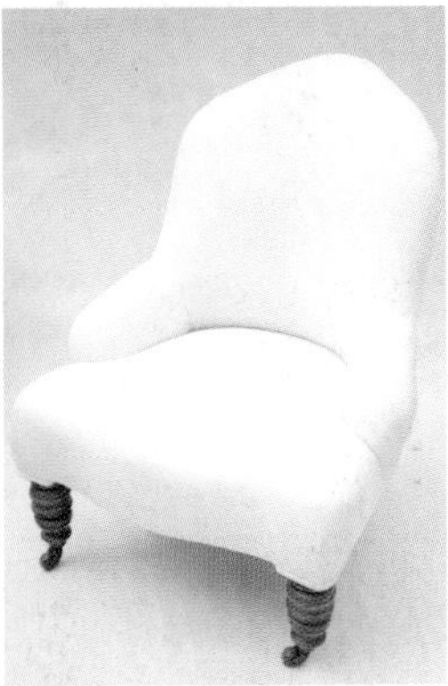

Nursing Chair

- *1890*

Victorian nursing chair upholstered in calico with mahogany turned legs and original porcelain castors.

- *117cm x 70cm*
- £420 • Myriad

Wing Chair ➤

- *circa 1730*

Queen Anne wing chair with padded seat and back, with scrolled arms, on square legs.

- *176cm x 78cm*
- £2,750 • Rod Wilson

George III Mahogany Chair ▲

- *1780*

A George III mahogany chair with shaped top rail and carved back splat with curved arms.

- *97.5cm x 57.5cm*
- £1,750 • C.H. Major

Carved Hall Chair ▲

- *1890*

Mahogany hall chair with carved top rail, slatted back, solid seat and turned decoration.

- *109cm x 46cm*
- £385 • Sign of the Times

Walnut and Beechwood Armchairs ▼

- *1760*

Pair of walnut and beechwood fauteuils. Stamped "Rovmaion", with continental needlework covers.

- *167cm x 60cm*
- £25,000 • O.F. Wilson

Dutch Walnut Marquetry Chairs ▼

- *1790*

One of a set of four Dutch walnut marquetry chairs with shaped back splat, cabriole legs, on claw and ball feet.

- *105cm x 55cm*
- £16,000 • Pimlico

Scottish Carved Dining Chairs ▼

- *1810*

A fine long set of 12 Scottish George III mahogany dining chairs including two armchairs. In excellent condition, with good colour and patination. Well carved bearing the influence of the leading furniture maker William Trotter.

- *height 79cm*
- £36,000 • Freshfords

Child's Chair ◀

- *circa 1820*

Provincial child's chair with good colour and patination.

- *87cm x 30cm x 31cm*
- £375 • Rod Wilson

East Anglian Reclining Chair

• ***18th century***
Unusual back-tilting elm chair, known as an East Anglian reclining chair.
• *117cm x 68cm x 43cm*
• £3,950 • **Lacquer Chest**

Laburnum Wood Chair

• ***1700***
An extremely rare chair of laburnum wood, having a tall back with scrolled arms and bulbous turned legs.
• *116cm x 53cm x 43cm*
• £7,850 • **M.W. & H.L.**

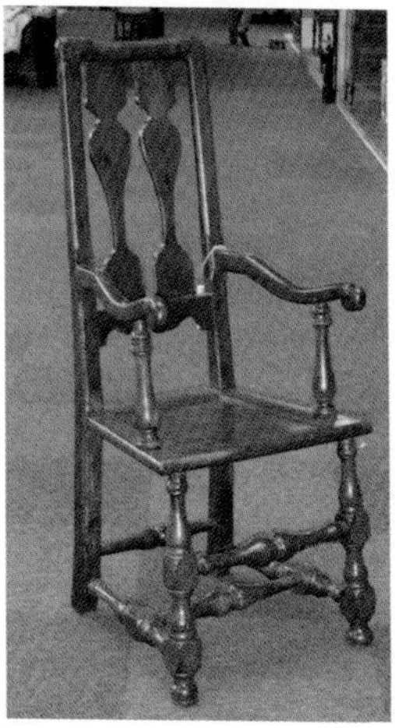

French Gilded Chairs

• ***circa 1890***
A pair of heavily gilded Louis XV-style bergères, with serpentine apron and escargot-style feet.
• *height 106cm*
• £5,850 • **Ranby Hall**

Flat Back Fauteuil

• ***circa 1780***
A French Louis XV flat back fauteuil, with serpentine drop-in seat, in moulded frame, on cabriole legs.
• *height 94cm*
• £7,500 • **Butchoff**

Satinwood Cane Chair

• ***circa 1900***
A Hepplewhite satinwood-style cane chair with painted decoration. Oval caned back and seat standing on turned legs.
• *143cm x 56cm x 52cm*
• £1,495 • **John Nicholas**

Shield Back Dining Chairs

• ***circa 1800***
A set of eight mahogany Hepplewhite-style shield back dining chairs, with two carvers.
• *height 80cm*
• £7,450 • **Great Grooms**

Mahogany Dining Chairs

• ***1835***
A set of six William IV mahogany dining chairs with finely carved backs on turned legs.
• *48cm x 45cm*
• £2,450 • **N.E. McAuliffe**

Victorian Curved Back Ship's Chair

• *circa 1880*

A Victorian walnut ship's chair, with curved back, circular padded seat on a cast iron base..

• *130cm x 57cm*

• £400 • **Tredantiques**

Biedermeier Armchairs

• *circa 1900*

Pair of Biedermeier-style birchwood armchairs, with inlays of mother of pearl, satinwood and rosewood.

• *149cm x 60cm x 52cm*

• £5,900 • **R. Cavendish**

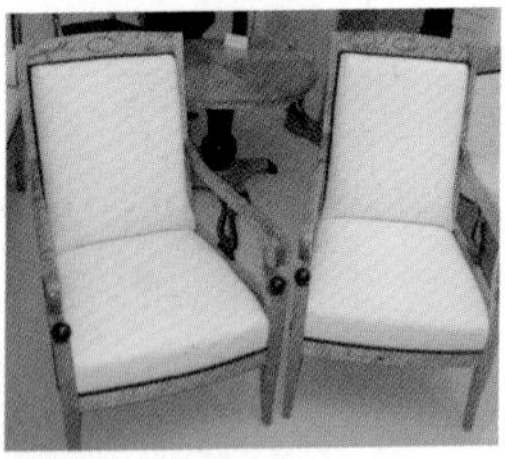

Oriental Elm Chairs

• *18th century*

A pair of eighteenth century Southern Chinese elm chairs with cane seats.

• *104cm x 56cm x 48cm*

• £3,500 • **Gerard Hawthorn**

Child's Correction Chair

• *1820*

A child's correction chair with turned ladder back and needlework seat, standing on splayed legs.

• *96cm x 33cm x 25cm*

• £1,100 • **Mac Humble**

Gripsholm Armchairs

• *circa 1930*

Pair of Swedish Gripsholm armchairs with original paint on ball feet.

• *height 78cm*

• £2,900 • **R. Cavendish**

Hepplewhite-Style Dining Chairs

• *circa 1890*

A set of mahogany Hepplewhite-style dining chairs which include eight single chairs and two arm chairs. With splayed backs, square moulded legs.

• *height 11ocm*

• £9,500 • **Butchoff**

William IV Nursing Chair

• *1830–37*

A William IV mahogany-framed nursing chair with deeply scrolled arms and arched legs.

• *100cm x 60cm*

• £2,200 • **John Clay**

Button-Back Chair

• *1830*
A William IV mahogany button-back armchair, with padded scroll arms, standing on cabriole legs on brass castors.
• *160cm x 70cm x 90cm*
• £2,350 • **Harpur Deardren**

Chinese Export Chair

• *circa 1860*
A rare Chinese chair made for the European market with balloon back and apron, heavily carved, raised on cabriole legs.
• *147cm x 56cm x 40cm*
• £975 • **Fay Orton**

Expert Tips

Chairs with silver gilt and gilt finishes are obviously subject to damage; slight distressing is acceptable but severe wear will considerably affect the price of the item.

Carved Oak Chairs

• *1870*
A set of six nineteenth-century English carved oak chairs, with heavily carved back splats, padded leather seats and turned legs, in the Flemish style.
• *160cm x 44cm*
• £850 • **Tredantiques**

Panelled Oak Chair

• *1640*
An oak arm chair with a carved panelled back and scrolled decoration on turned legs.
• *108cm x 61cm*
• £4,950 • **Peter Bunting**

Open-Fronted Giltwood Chairs

• *1850*
A pair of giltwood open-fronted bergères with carved decoration, on cabriole and knurled feet.
• *67cm x 68cm*
• £6,500 • **Ranby Hall**

Empire-Style Armchairs

• *circa 1890*
Pair of Empire-style Swedish mahogany armchairs with ormolu mounts.
• *height 83cm*
• £6,500 • **R. Cavendish**

Rosewood Dining Chairs

• *1820*
A Regency rosewood dining chair, one of a set of six, the concave top rail with fruitwood inlay, heavily gadrooned, on turned legs.
• *48cm x 47cm*
• £3,995 • **Harpur Deardren**

Balloon-Back Chairs ▼
- *circa 1850*
A set of six nineteenth-century
walnut balloon-back dining
chairs with carved scrolled oval
backs on cabriole legs.
- *89cm x 44cm*
- £2,995   • Great Grooms

Painted Child's Chair ▼
- *19th century*
A child's painted ash chair with a
high straight comb back, standing
on turned tapered legs.
- *83cm x 30cm*
- £3,600   • Paul Hopwell

Lacquered Elbow Chair ➤
- *19th century*
A black lacquer chair with a
shaped back rest, rush seat, comb
back and slender doric legs.
- *89cm x 52cm x 48cm*
- £498   • Lacquer Chest

Reclining Chair ▲
- *1860*
Reclining chair with scrolled
arms and turned legs on original
brass castors with original leather
upholstery.
- *101cm x 56cm x 65cm*
- £1,200   • Lacquer Chest

Victorian Bedroom Chair ▲
- *1880*
A Victorian chair with cane seat
painted a soft green, decorated
with red autumn leaves, standing
on sabre legs.
- *81cm x 46cm x 38cm*
- £340   • Lacquer Chest

Nursing Chair ▲
- *1910*
An Edwardian rosewood inlaid
nursing chair with lyre back,
standing on square tapered legs
with a splayed foot.
- *height 74cm*
- £895   • Great Grooms

Chippendale Elbow Chair ▲
- *1870*
A Chippendale chinoiserie-style
ribbon-back chair with scrolled
cabriole legs on claw and ball
feet.
- *107cm x 64cm x 49cm*
- £1,500   • J. Fox

Chaises Longues & Day Beds

Mahogany Chaise Longue ➤

- ***circa* 1830**

Fine William IV mahogany covered chaise longue.

- *length 1.47m*
- £8,500 • **Butchoff**

Victorian Chaise Longue ⮝

- ***19th century***

With pierced and scrolling leaf decoration, on cabriole legs.

- *height 96cm*
- £1,675 • **Castlegate**

Walnut Settee ➤

- ***circa* 1860**

English, canvas with button back, standing on cabriole legs.

- *length 2.2m*
- £4,950 • **S. & A. Thompson**

William IV Day Bed ⮜

- ***circa* 1835**

William IV rosewood daybed.

- *length 1.84m*
- £5,500 • **Butchoff**

Expert Tips

The condition of the framework of a chaise longue is all-important. The condition of the upholstery is also important, but only in so far as it is very expensive to replace. The novelty of springs led restorers of the late 19th and early 20th centuries to use them rather than taut webbing in reupholstery. A bad idea.

Mahogany Day Bed ➤

- ***circa* 1830**

Cuban mahogany day bed with bronze engraving on the lower side panel. In excellent condition.

- *length 1.9m*
- £1,900 • **Pillows**

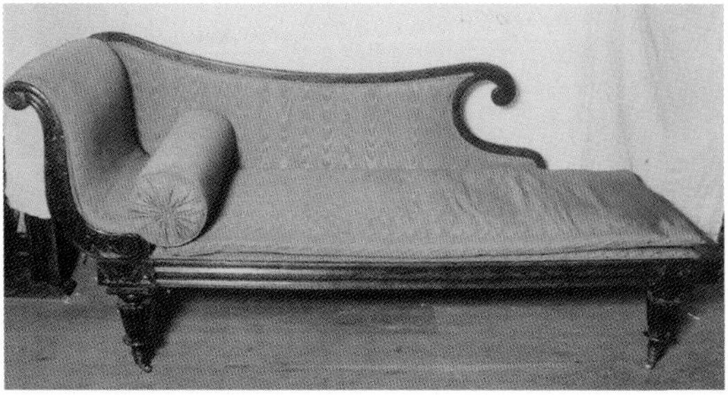

English Chaise Longue ➤

- ***circa* 1820**

A Regency green watered silk faux rosewood chaise longue with carving.

- *length 1.88m*
- £2,900 • **Mora & Upham**

Chests of Drawers & Commodes

Bow Chest

- ***circa* 1850**

A Victorian mahogany bow-fronted chest of drawers.

- *height 89cm*
- £1,650 • **C. Preston**

Chest on Stand

- ***circa* 1710**

A fine chest on original stand with exceptional patina.

- *height 1.32m*
- £7,000 • **Raffety**

Oak Chest

- ***circa* 1820**

A 19th-century oak chest of drawers with brass, swan-necked handles and bracket feet.

- *height 1.04m*
- £750 • **Fulham**

Channel Islands Tallboy

- ***circa* 1800**

Beautifully faded mahogany with shell inlay and original brass.

- *height 2.05m*
- **£14,500**
- **M. Wakelin & H. Linfield**

Mahogany Tallboy

- ***circa* 1825**

A Swedish tallboy of unusually narrow form, with gilded mounts and lion's-paw feet.

- *height 1.36m*
- £4,500 • **Cavendish**

Linen Press

- ***circa* 1860**

Victorian mahogany linen press with oval panel doors.

- *height 2.31m*
- £4,450 • **Ranby Hall**

Expert Tips

It is highly advantageous to the value of a chest of drawers to have its original handles. Check inside a drawer to see if there are any holes from handles of a previous incarnation.

Step Commode

- ***circa* 1830**

William IV commode in the form of library steps, with hinged compartment, on four turned legs.

- *height 79cm*
- £950 • **Castlegate**

Chest of Drawers
- *circa 1725*

George I figured walnut chest of drawers with slide and original handles on moulded bracket feet.
- *height 83cm*
- £16,000 • Norman Adams

Bombé Chest
- *circa 1780*

European bombé-fronted chest of drawers and linen press.
- *height 2.2m*
- £6,500 • L. & E. Krekovic

Chest on Chest
- *circa 1760*

Mahogany chest on chest, the top with moulded cornice.
- *height 1.79m*
- £4,200 • Old Cinema

Chest on Stand
- *circa 1770*

Oak chest with walnut veneer, with drawers of graduated sizes, on later oak base with serpentine stretchers and turned legs.
- *height 1.5m*
- £3,900 • Angel

Tallboy
- *circa 1760*

A George III mahogany tallboy, with chamfered corners, with slide, on bracket feet.
- *height 1.8m*
- £6,500 • Terence Morse

Inlaid Commode
- *circa 1890*

A late 19th-century, inlaid Louis XV-style serpentine commode with fruitwood and satinwood marquetry and ormolu mounts, on splayed legs.
- *height 85cm*
- £1,250 • Youlls

Marriage Coffer
- *circa 1724*

A Swedish coffer in pale oak with original paint and iron strapwork.
- *length 1.53m*
- £3,800 • Riverbank

Oak Chest of Drawers

- *circa 1880*

An oak graduated chest of drawers with pearl escutcheons and circular brass handles.

- *height 84cm*
- £750 • **Fulham**

Linen Press

- *circa 1864*

Flame mahogany linen press with moulded decoration to the doors.

- *height 2.31m*
- £4,450 • **Ranby Hall**

Bachelor Chest

- *circa 1705*

An unusual, small Queen Anne walnut bachelor chest, with original mounts.

- *height 81cm*
- £80,000 • **Norman Adams**

Bow-Fronted Commode

- *circa 1800*

A lift-top commode on splayed feet with replacement mounts.

- *height 66cm*
- £420 • **Albany**

Expert Tips

Early veneer was hand-cut and will not be of a regular thickness. Machine-cut veneer will be thinner and uniform. You can see the thickness on the edges of the drawers.

Dressing Chest

- *circa 1760*

A dressing chest, in mahogany, with top drawer fitted with original mirror and shaving box.

- *height 82cm*
- £3,250 • **Christopher Preston**

China Trade Chest

- *circa 1820*

A China trade chest of amboyna, with military-style handles.

- *height 1.01m*
- £14,500
- **M. Wakelin & H. Linfield**

Directoire Commode

- *circa 1790*

A directoire French commode.

- *height 83cm*
- £16,500
- **M. Wakelin & H. Linfield**

Oak Coffer

- ***17th century***

A 17th-century oak coffer with organic and geometric carving, on bracket feet.

- *height 99cm*
- £1,200 • Angel

Oak Chest of Drawers

- ***circa 1680***

A 17th-century oak chest of drawers with applied geometric moulding, the whole on stile feet.

- *height 84cm*
- £7,750 • Angel

Wellington Chest

- ***circa 1870***

A Victorian, seven-drawer Wellington chest, in mahogany.

- *height 1.28m*
- £2,900 • Old Cinema

Mule Chest

- ***circa 1700***

Oak mule chest with original lozenge carving and two drawers.

- *length 1.04m*
- £1,650 • Red Lion

Italian Commode

- ***circa 1750***

Serpentine-fronted commode with profuse painted decoration.

- *height 86cm*
- £7,500 • Lynda Franklin

Chest of Drawers

- ***circa 1790***

A mahogany, serpentine-fronted chest of drawers with satinwood cross-banding and splayed feet.

- *height 91cm*
- £5,850 • Harvey

Expert Tips

It is unusual to find an English commode in the "bombé" shape – the swollen, curved design much-loved by European furniture makers.

Wellington Chest

- ***circa 1860***

An exceptionally large, Victorian walnut Wellington chest.

- *height 2m*
- £5,500 • Harvey

Lacquer Commode

- *circa 1860*

English bombé commode, chinoiserie painted and lacquered.

- *height 92cm*
- £8,000 • **David Ford**

Italian Commode

- *circa 1895*

Venetian amboyna commode on splayed legs with scrolled feet.

- *height 92cm*
- £4,850 • **Lamberty**

Large Chest of Drawers

- *circa 1800*

A George III chest of drawers with original brass handles on splayed, bracket feet.

- *height 1.2m*
- £1,100 • **Castlegate**

Bombé Commode

- *circa 1876*

An Italian, bombé serpentine commode in figured burr walnut and mounted on cabriole legs.

- *height 83cm*
- £4,250
- **M. Wakelin & H. Linfield**

Italian Commode

- *circa 1785*

A double bow-fronted Italian commode, made in the 18th century and painted in the early 19th, with découpage decoration. (Découpage is the art of using paper cutouts to decorate furniture and accessories such as boxes and trays, after they have been sanded and painted. The finished object which has been so decorated looks and feels, after the application of a protective sealant, like fine enamel).

- *height 78cm*
- £5,850 • **Browns**

Chest on Chest

- *circa 1760*

Figured mahogany chest on chest with original brass handles.

- *height 2.1m*
- £10,400 • **Chambers**

Expert Tips

Furniture with a wax finish should be polished no more frequently than every few weeks or so. To be properly protective, the surface needs time to harden between polishes.

Miniature Chest

- *circa 1880*

A Cuban mahogany miniature chest of drawers with rounded corners and plinth base.

- *height 75cm*
- £1,650 • **Walpole**

Spanish Oak Coffer

• *circa 1680–1700*
Spanish coffer with elaborate geometric carving, standing on a square base.
• *59cm x 137cm x 52cm*
• £2,750 • Rod Wilson

Margot Fonteyn's Chest of Drawers

• *1820*
An unusual decorated chest of drawers. Provenance: the Prima Ballerina, Margot Fonteyn.
• *97cm x 103cm*
• £5,250 • Pimlico Antiques

Small Carved Coffer

• *circa 1680*
A well-carved late seventeenth century oak coffer in good original condition.
• *53cm x 108cm x 46cm*
• £1,400 • Rod Wilson

Heavily Carved Coffer

• *circa 1680*
Oak coffer with bold carving and superb colouring and patination.
• *195cm x 144cm x 47cm*
• £1,650 • Rod Wilson

Large Mahogany Chest of Drawers

• *circa 1760*
A rare oversized mahogany chest of drawers with exceptional colour and patination, raised on feet.
• *119cm x 94cm x 52cm*
• £2,450 • Rod Wilson

Mahogany Chest of Drawers

• *circa 1800*
Mahogany chest of drawers with five long drawers with brass fittings, standing on bracket feet.
• *118cm x 107cm x 56cm*
• £1,975 • Rod Wilson

Oak Coffer

• *circa 1670*
An oak coffer carved with a central rose and foliate designs. Standing on straight square legs.
• *45cm x 105cm x 75cm*
• £1,295 • Rod Wilson

English Oak Coffer

- *circa 1760*

An English oak chest with three carved panels.

- *75cm x 118cm x 49cm*
- £575 • Tredantiques

Chest on Stand

- *circa 1750*

A walnut and feather-banded chest on stand. The stand has an arched apron on turned legs with serpentine stretcher on ball feet.

- *60cm x 40.7cm x 23.5cm*
- £4,995 • Great Grooms

Oak and Mahogany Chest

- *1790*

Mahogany chest of drawers with oak and mahogany banding and brass mounts on bracket feet.

- *92cm x 80cm x 50cm*
- £2,650 • Rod Wilson

English Mule Chest

- *circa 1700*

An English oak mule chest with three carved panels above two short drawers with floral carvings.

- *80cm x 125cm x 52cm*
- £1,000 • Tredantiques

Oak Plank Chest

- *circa 1630*

An oak plank chest of exceptionally small proportions with good original carving and original iron lock.

- *50cm x 80cm x 33cm*
- £1,850 • Rod Wilson

Mahogany Wellington Chest

- *1860*

A fine flame mahogany Wellington chest with moulded top, having five drawers with original turned handles, on a plinth base.

- *120cm x 67cm x 40cm*
- £2,985 • Old Cinema

Chest-on-Chest

- *circa 1780*

A George III mahogany chest-on-chest with moulded cornice, brass escutcheons and handles, raised on bracket feet.

- *185cm x 114cm x 53cm*
- £6,250 • Rod Wilson

Dutch Chest of Drawers ▲
- ***mid-18th century***

Dutch mahogany chest of drawers, of serpentine form with oval brass mounts.
- *78cm x 75cm x 47cm*
- £7,800 • **M. Luther**

Louis XVI Commode ▲
- ***1790***

Louis XVI commode with brass moulding and gallery on a white marble top.
- *88cm x 110cm x 55cm*
- £10,000 • **O.F. Wilson**

William and Mary Chest ▲
- ***1690***

Rare William and Mary chest of drawers in walnut. The top, sides and drawer fronts decorated with reserves of floral marquetry. Raised on original bun feet.
- *94cm x 96cm x 60cm*
- £48,000 • **M.W. & H.L.**

Figured Mahogany Chest ▲
- ***19th century***

Figured mahogany and pine chest with banding and graduated drawers, raised on bun feet.
- *120cm x 120cm*
- £770 • **Drummonds**

Campaign Chest ▼
- ***early 19th century***

A colonial rosewood chest consisting of two sections with four drawers on bracket feet.
- *93cm x 77cm x 35.5cm*
- £3,200 • **M. Luther**

Victorian Chest ▲
- ***19th century***

Victorian mahogany chest of drawers with turned handles and four drawers resting on bun feet.
- *130cm x 120cm*
- £825 • **Drummonds**

George III Chest of Drawers ▲
- ***circa 1760***

Rare English George III oak chest of drawers with oval brass mounts, on shaped bracket feet.
- *77cm x 76cm x 44cm*
- £4,450 • **M. Luther**

Pine Chest of Drawers

- ***1900s***

A pine chest having three tiers of drawers with scrolled decoration, brass fittings, standing on bun feet.

- *95cm x 58cm x 77cm*
- £400 • Old School

English Blanket Box

- ***1900s***

An English well-figured pine chest in restored condition on turned bun feet.

- *51cm x 99cm x 59cm*
- £225 • Old School

Blanket Box

- ***1899s***

Nineteenth-century pine chest with scrolled apron, standing on bracket feet.

- *104cm x 49cm x 52cm*
- £220 • Old School

Biedermeier Chest of Drawers

- ***circa 1820***

A German Biedermeier chest of drawers made from birchwood with ebonised architectural columns.

- *78cm x 109cm x 53cm*
- £5,900 • R. Cavendish

Three-Drawered Chest

- ***1900s***

A pine chest of drawers consisting of three deep drawers with porcelain bun handles with carved moulding to the side.

- *127cm x 102cm x 63cm*
- £495 • Old School

Expert Tips

To check that the dovetailing is original on a chest of drawers, pull out all of the drawers.

Mahogany Chest-on-Chest

- ***1780***

Chinese Chippendale-style, mahogany chest-on-chest with blind fretwork and chamfered corners on shaped bracket feet.

- *190cm x 120cm*
- £5,900 • Midwinter

Rosewood Chest on Chest

- ***1870***

An English Victorian rosewood chest-on-chest with satinwood banding and oval brass mounts, on a plinth base.

- *194cm x 104cm x 49cm*
- £5,850 • Ranby Hall

George III Chest-on-Chest

- *circa 1812*

A George III figured mahogany chest-on-chest, with chamfered corners, dentil course and brass mounts on plain bracket feet.

- *71.5cm x 41cm*
- £3,850 • Great Grooms

Rosewood Commode

- *18th century*

A Swedish rosewood commode with a marble top and two long drawers below, standing on tapered legs with oval brass mounts.

- *88cm x 112cm x 57cm*
- £7,400 • Heytesbury

Carved Mule Chest

- *18th century*

An oak mule chest with three carved panels with two drawers below with original handles, on plain straight legs.

- *height 70cm*
- £1,195 • Great Grooms

Kingwood Commode

- *circa 1740*

French Regency kingwood commode with ormolu mounts and rouge royale serpentine marble top.

- *85cm x 118cm x 60cm*
- £22,000 • Guinevere

Mahogany Tall Boy

- *1750*

English mahogany tall boy with moulded dentil cornice, seven graduated drawers with brass fittings, standing on shaped bracket feet.

- *195cm x 107cm x 55cm*
- £11,700 • M.W. & H.L.

William and Mary Chest of Drawers

- *1690*

An excellent example of William-and-Mary-period chest of drawers with two short and three long drawers on turned bun feet. The whole in oyster laburnum with broad cross banding to the sides, top and drawer fronts.

- *84cm x 91cm x 56cm*
- £24,000 • M.W. & H.L.

Swedish Bombé Commode

- *circa 1890*

A Swedish bombé commode with gilded brass mounts made from walnut, raised on splayed feet.

- *82cm x 93cm x 52cm*
- £2,250 • S. Hatchwell

Davenports

Burr Walnut Davenport ➤

• *circa 1850*
Decorated with boxwood marquetry with Wellington door-closing mechanism.
• *height 84cm*
• £5,400 • **Judy Fox**

William IV Davenport ➤

• *circa 1830*
In rosewood, sitting on carved bun feet with castors. With tan leather writing surface and brass heart insignia on the rail.
• *height 90cm*
• £2,950 • **F. Beck**

Mahogany Davenport ➤

• *circa 1860*
With swivel top, brass gallery and fitted interior.
• *height 85cm*
• £1,950 • **Youlls**

Regency Davenport ➤

• *circa 1810*
Rosewood davenport with drawers on the side, side pillars and a mustard green inlay.
• *height 85cm*
• £1,950 • **Tower Bridge**

Burr Elm Davenport ➤

• *circa 1880*
Burr elm davenport with lift top and brass gallery.
• *height 85cm*
• £8,700 • **Butchoff**

Walnut Davenport ➤

• *circa 1860*
With secret pen tray, cabriole legs, leaf decoration and brass gallery. The whole on bun feet.
• *height 84cm*
• £1,650 • **Castlegate**

Desks

Pedestal Desk

- *circa 1800*

A mahogany pedestal desk with original brass handles, raised on bun feet.

- *76cm x 135cm x 72cm*
- £1,800 • John Clay

Kneehole Desk

- *1880*

A small oak and mahogany kneehole desk with cupboard, one long drawer, and three drawers either side of the kneehole.

- *77cm x 89cm x 44cm*
- £995 • Great Grooms

Oak Kneehole Desk

- *1727–60*

A George II-style kneehole desk made from oak with brass handles and central cupboard, resting on bracket feet.

- *height 79cm*
- £2,650 • Great Grooms

Tambour Desk

- *circa 1900*

A French mahogany tambour desk with Bonn retailer's label. Including sliding and rotating compartmented drawer.

- *144cm x 158cm x 90cm*
- £14,500 • S. Hatchwell

Biedermeier Writing Desk

- *circa 1830*

A mahogany Biedermeier writing desk with galleried top and shaped kneehole, on turned legs.

- *77cm x 143cm x 69cm*
- £3,850 • Ranby Hall

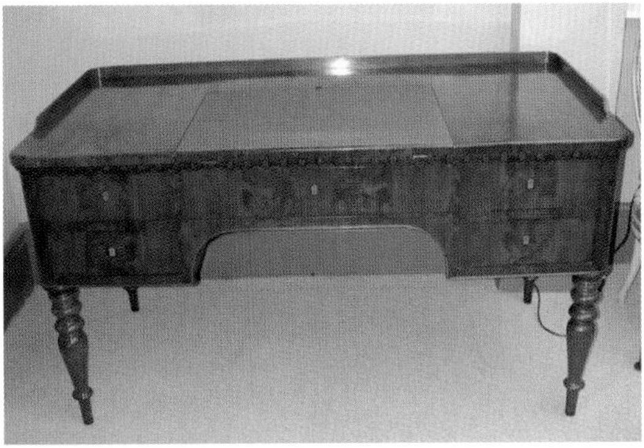

Mahogany Pedestal Desk

- *1860*

A nineteenth-century mahogany pedestal desk with three tiers of drawers either side of the kneehole on a moulded plinth base.

- *78cm x 120cm x 70cm*
- £3,450 • Brown

Expert Tips

The eighteenth-century small kneehole desk has always been in great demand; some examples in walnut command high sums. However, some late nineteenth-century copies are also valuable.

Partners' Desk

- *circa 1840*

A mid-19th-century figured mahogany desk with frieze drawers. Replacement leather inlay. On shaped plinth base.

- *height 78cm*
- £2,000 • **Spencer**

Lady's Writing Desk

- *circa 1890*

Walnut gothic-style lady's writing desk with two doors enclosing open shelves with leather inset writing top.

- *height 67cm*
- £695 • **Fulham**

Expert Tips

Tooled leather panels came in at the end of the 19th century. Good replacement panels are not detrimental.

Lady's Desk

- *circa 1880*

A rosewood lady's desk, with boxwood inlay, decorated with penwork to a floral design, with leather insert. Standing on eight tapering legs, with splayed feet and castors.

- *height 94cm*
- £3,600 • **Judy Fox**

Kneehole Desk

- *circa 1740*

A rare kneehole desk in solid cherrywood with good patina.

- *height 89cm*
- £2,750 • **Red Lion**

Reading Table

- *circa 1785*

A George III satinwood reading table of simple lines, with prop-up reading and writing surface and two drawers with original ceramic handles, on tapering legs with brass castors.

- *height 74.5cm*
- £15,000 • **Norman Adams**

Partners' Desk

- *circa 1780*

A large, mahogany partners' desk with frieze drawers and plain curved brass handles, all raised on shaped bracket feet.

- *height 77cm*
- £2,600 • **Spencer**

Cylinder-Top Desk

• ***circa* 1870**
Victorian cylinder-top desk with various compartments, pull-out writing flap and drawers.
• *height 1.26m*
• £3,500 • **Old Cinema**

William IV Desk

• ***circa* 1825**
Mahogany drop-leaf pembroke desk with one dummy drawer on back and real one on front. On a turned base.
• *height 73cm*
• £2,600 • **L. & E. Kreckovic**

Writing Desk

•***circa* 1920**
Mahogany Hepplewhite writing desk with brass-bound and leather top on carved cabriole legs.
• *height 73cm*
• £695 • **Fulham Antiques**

French Cylinder Desk

• ***circa* 1780**
Walnut cylinder desk on square legs with drawers above and below and pull-out writing flap.
• *height 1.27m*
• £5,500 • **Kenneth Harvey**

Oak Desk

• ***circa* 1850**
Partners' desk with four drawers to each pedestal and three-drawer frieze. Original brass handles.
• *height 74cm*
• £3,800 • **Terence Morse**

Roll-Top Desk

• ***circa* 1880**
A rare English Victorian roll-top desk in solid mahogany, signed Hobb & Co, with fitted locks and handles.
• *height 1.2m*
• £1,950 • **Chris Newland**

Expert Tips

Large desks were cut down when smaller desks became fashionable. Look for the repositioning of drawer handles.

Birch Desk

• ***circa* 1830**
Unusual satinwood, birch and ebony line-inlaid desk with a rising lid and well-fitted interior.
• *height 95cm*
• £1,450 • **M.J. Bowdery**

Chinese Writing Table

- ***late 19th century***

Rosewood bombé/serpentine-shaped writing table.

- *height 1.16m*
- **£1,950** • **John Clay**

French Desk

- ***circa 1850***

A 19th-century French painted beech and pinewood desk, with curved drawer on central opening and bracket feet.

- *width 1.92m*
- **£3,000** • **Oonagh Black**

Fruitwood Country Desk

- ***19th century***

In fruitwood with cabriole legs and three drawers.

- *height 77cm*
- **£1,835** • **I. & J. L. Brown**

Walnut Desk

- ***circa 1840***

A figured walnut pedestal desk with rounded corners and heavy moulding. Original knob handles.

- *height 78cm*
- **£5,500** • **Ian Spencer**

Mahogany Desk

- ***circa 1920***

Early 20th-century mahogany desk in the George III manner. The top is inlaid with calf leather and decorated with gold tooling.

- *height 79cm*
- **£1,500** • **Westland & Co**

Expert Tips

Handles and feet are the most obvious and the easiest aids in dating a piece of furniture. Unfortunately, they are also the easiest parts to alter.

Lady's Writing Table

- ***circa 1880***

A Victorian mahogany lady's writing table with seven drawers and ebonised stringing. Standing on tapered legs.

- *length 1.22m*
- **£1,995** • **Antique Warehouse**

Satinwood Kidney-Shaped Desk

• *circa 1900*

A good quality satinwood kidney desk having five drawers with original handles and good locks. All keys are supplied. Having a crossbanded and leather top standing on string inlaid legs with splayed feet.

• *75cm x 120cm x 65cm*

• **£3,500** • **S. Hatchwell**

Swedish Writing Desk

• *circa 1810*

Swedish Empire mahogany writing desk with drawers and decorated brass handles.

• *75cm x 94cm x 51cm*

• **£3,900** • **R. Cavendish**

Rosewood Desk

• *circa 1870s*

Small Victorian rosewood desk with a writing slope concealing fitted interior and original brass handles on cabriole legs.

• *93cm x 55cm*

• **£1,800** • **Sign of the Times**

Lacquer Kneehole Desk

• *circa 1880s*

Black lacquer and gilt kneehole desk, of colonial influence.

• *103cm x 103cm*

• **£1,700** • **Sign of the Times**

Chippendale-Style Writing Table

• *circa 1900*

A Chippendale-style writing table comprising one long drawer and two side drawers on either side of the kneehole. All drawers are fitted with drop handles. The whole is raised on architectural carved legs.

• *77cm x 126cm x 60cm*

• **£4,950** • **Brown**

Dining Tables

Regency Dining Table ➤

• ***1820***

A fine Regency mahogany extending dining table made by Thomas Wilkinson of London, with a scissor-action lazy tongs mechanism for extending the table.

• *height 86cm*

• **£1,765** • **Freshfords**

Expert Tips

When looking at a dining table, consider whether your current set of chairs are the correct height for the table you wish to purchase. When considering D- end tables, always inspect the condition of the leaves and their colour, as these leaves have often been stored and appear darker than the rest of the table. Here again, it is important that the patina of the dining surface of the table is without cracks or gouges, and the surface should be level and not warped or wavy.

French Dining Table ⮟

• ***late 19th century***

French fruitwood provincial farmhouse table.

• *76cm x 200cm*

• **£1,950** • **Old Cinema**

Mahogany Three-Leaved Dining Table ⮟

• ***1885***

Victorian mahogany dining table with three leaves on turned legs with original castors.

• *74cm x 122cm*

• **£4,250** • **Old Cinema**

Extendable Dining Table ⮝

• ***circa 1870***

A Victorian mahogany table with baluster fluted legs, extendable to 300cm.

• *74cm x 138cm x 150cm*

• **£3,500** • **Tredantiques**

Victorian Dining Table ⮝

• ***1837–1901***

Victorian dining table in its original condition, with figured mahogany.

• *height 74cm*

• **£3,750** • **Old Cinema**

Five-Leaf Table

• ***circa* 1830**
A circular, figured Cuban mahogany dining table with five leaves on reeded legs, extending to seat twelve people.
• *diameter 145cm*
• **£9,800** • **Luther & Goodwin**

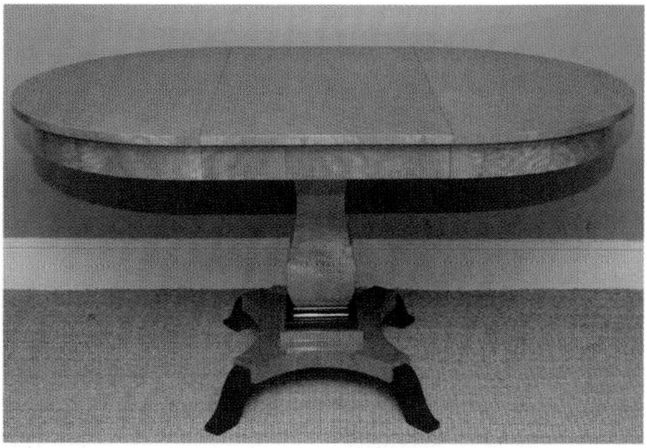

Extending Table

• ***circa* 1920**
Swedish birchwood extending table with ebonised feet.
• *length 2.63m (extended)*
• **£4,900** • **Cavendish**

Drop-Leaf Table

• ***circa* 1825**
George IV mahogany drop-leaf dining table on six turned legs.
• *width 1.67m*
• **£4,300** • **L. & E. Kreckovic**

> **Expert Tips**
>
> *Drop-leaf tables rarely have tops that are inlaid or crossbanded. This form of decoration will almost always have been added at a later date.*

Walnut Dining Table

• ***circa* 1880**
Burr-walnut oval Victorian tilt-top dining table on pillared triform base with carved feet and ceramic castors.
• *height 87cm*
• **£1,750** • **Fulham**

Tip-up Table

• ***circa* 1825**
Mahogany tip-up dining table from the William IV period.
• *width 1.4m*
• **£2,500** • **L. & E. Kreckovic**

French Farmhouse Table

• ***circa* 1890**
Large table with pine top and turned and tapered walnut legs.
• *length 2.4m*
• **£2,000** • **Gabrielle de Giles**

Doors

Metal-Studded Door ▼
- *circa 1885*
Substantial Gothic oak, metal-studded door, with six panels and Gothic tracery.
- £2,450
- Drummonds

Teardrop Loft Door ▼
- *circa 1870*
Game-larder or loft door of possible French origin.
- *height 2.34m*
- £1,475
- Annette Puttnam

Pine Overdoor ▲
- *circa 1890*
Carved pine overdoor in the George I style.
- *height 77.5cm*
- £450
- Westland & Co

Double Doors ▲
- *circa 1910*
A pair of six-panelled mahogany doors with brass furniture.
- *height 2.8m*
- £3,500
- Ian Spencer

Italian Double Doors ▼
- *circa 1790*
A pair of giltwood and ivory painted double doors, centred by jasper panels.
- *height 2.95m*
- £15,000
- Westland & Co

Carved Oak Doorway ▼
- *circa 1850*
A finely carved oak doorway in the Venetian renaissance manner.
- *height 2.49m*
- £3,200
- Westland & Co

Baroque-Style Overdoor ◄
- *circa 1890*
A carved wood overdoor in the baroque manner.
- *height 1m*
- £1,600
- Westland & Co

Victorian Mahogany Door

- *circa 1840s*

Early Victorian mahogany four-panelled door with original brass fittings.

- *200cm x 75cm*
- £2,100 • Drummonds

Gothic Oak Doors

- *late 19th century*

Oak-panelled doors with gothic tracery, original brass fittings and stained glass windows.

- *101cm x 226cm*
- £850 • Drummonds

Linenfold Door

- *18th century*

Light oak linenfold panelled door.

- *300cm x 120cm*
- £1,350 • Drummonds

Indian Panelled Doors

- *18th century*

Antique panelled doors with elaborate strapwork and floral decorated brass.

- *192cm x 120cm*
- £1,250 • Gordon Reece

Victorian Slatted Doors

- *19th century*

A pair of Victorian oak-slatted doors with original scrolled iron hinges and fittings.

- *165cm x 219cm*
- £1,475 • Drummonds

Panelled Mahogany Door

- *19th century*

Mahogany six panelled door, with no fittings and the original "PRIVATE" sign on the front.

- *200cm x 90cm*
- £875 • Drummonds

Expert Tips

Church doors with their elaborate iron hinges are sought after by garden designers for use within a garden scheme.

Dressers

Cupboard
- ***18th century***

Housekeeper's cupboard with original handles and brassware.
- *height 1.95m*
- £5,800 • **Riverbank**

Display Case
- ***19th century***

Queen Anne-style with lattice work and floral decoration.
- *height 2.06m*
- £5,850 • **Ranby Hall**

Storage Cupboard
- ***circa 1820***

Northern Swedish cupboard with typical rural profile doors. Good carving to the top and base.
- *height 2.01m*
- £3,200 • **Aberg**

Charles II Cupboard
- ***circa 1680***

Oak court cupboard with heraldic central panel.
- *height 1.64m*
- £3,850 • **Angel**

Buffet de Corps
- ***circa 1790***

Rare dresser in yew wood with three tiers of shelves above a base with three drawers.
- *height 2m*
- £5,950 • **Red Lion**

Walnut Dresser
- ***circa 1890***

Aesthetic movement dresser, with panels of birds, highlighting, amboyna back and acorn finials.
- *height 1.72m*
- £1,250 • **Travers**

Louis XVI Dresser
- ***18th century***

Swedish Gustavian dresser painted in off-white.
- *length 2m*
- £7,500 • **Cavendish**

Oak Dresser

• *circa 1790*

With cupboards, shelving and drawers. Replacement knobs.

• *height 1.89m*

• £1,750 • **Albany**

French Cupboard

• *18th century*

Cupboard in oak serpentine frieze with floral carving.

• *length 1.69m*

• £1,200 • **Lynda Franklin**

Welsh Deuddiarw

• *circa 1740*

Rare cupboard with small proportions. Cupboards above two drawers and cupboards below.

• *height 1.8m*

• £5,950 • **Red Lion**

French Buffet d'Accord

• *circa 1800*

Cherrywood buffet with carved panelled doors, a chapeau cornice and escargot legs.

• *height 2.47m*

• £7,500 • **Oonagh Black**

Cherrywood Cabinet

• *circa 1720*

French provincial cabinet with moulded frieze and square feet.

• *height 2.17m*

• £3,750 • **Albany**

Expert Tips

Before buying a dresser, check that all the drawers match each other in terms of appearance and manufacture (dovetailing etc.). Replacement parts are very detrimental to desirability.

Chiffonier

• *circa 1830*

A late Regency, two-door mahogany chiffonier.

• *height 1.26m*

• £1,650 • **Castlegate**

Cabriole Leg Dresser

• *circa 1760*

Base in good original condition with replaced handles.

• *height 83cm*

• £5,950 • **Red Lion**

Welsh Dresser

- *circa 1740*

A Welsh oak dresser with three shelves flanked by panelled spice cupboards, standing on bracket feet and brass fittings.

- *186cm x 136cm x 49cm*
- £9,500 • **Rod Wilson**

Welsh Deuddiarw

- *circa 1740*

An original eighteenth century Welsh deuddiarw. The upper section with cornice above panelled cupboards.

- *177cm x 104cm x 52cm*
- £5,950 • **Rod Wilson**

Victorian Mahogany Chiffonier

- *1850*

Victorian mahogany chiffonier with long drawer above two panelled cupboards, standing on small bun feet.

- *91cm x 42cm x 104cm*
- £590 • **Tredantiques**

Court Cupboard

- *1691*

A Westmorland oak court cupboard, with overhanging cornice and turned decoration with turned wood handles and good patina.

- *160cm x 133cm x 56cm*
- £7,950 • **Peter Bunting**

French Mahogany Dresser

- *1860*

A fine Victorian figured mahogany dresser with two shelves, the back having a scallop design, with two drawers and panelled cupboards below, standing on bun feet.

- *169cm x 123cm x 46cm*
- £1,800 • **Tredantiques**

English Oak Dresser

- *circa 1760*

An oak dresser with carved frieze above three shelves with a solid back, the dresser base with three tiers of drawers flanked by two moulded cupboard doors.

- *191cm x 181cm x 59cm*
- £5,500 • **Rod Wilson**

Glazed Pine Dresser

- *1900s*

Pine dresser consisting of three glazed doors with shelving above a pine base, with two shallow drawers and panelled cupboard with brass fittings.

- *128cm x 98cm x 55cm*
- £700 • Old School

Decorated Court Cupboard

- *1760*

An oak court cupboard with moulded cornice above a plain frieze with drop finials, the two-cupboard door flanking an arched panel.

- *166cm x 146cm x 61cm*
- £6,850 • Rod Wilson

Expert Tips

Back boards of dressers and court cupboards should be affixed by old iron clout nails, and the boards should be handworked, rustic and irregular.

Buffet de Corps

- *18th century*

A rare yew wood buffet de corps with three tiers of shelves above a base with three drawers and two cupboard doors.

- *20cm x 137cm*
- £5,950 • Red Lion

Carved Oak Dresser

- *late 17th century*

English oak dresser with heavily carved sides and doors, standing on straight square feet with iron fittings.

- *131cm x 172cm x 56cm*
- £2,500 • Tredantiques

Deuddiarw Carved Cupboard

- *1760*

An oak deuddiarw carved dresser with good patina, with carved pediment and drop finials above two cupboards, three drawers and panel doors.

- *167cm x 143cm*
- £6,850 • Red Lion

Painted French Dresser

- *18th century*

French painted pine dresser with two glass doors and panelled cupboards below, on a square base.

- *height 183cm*
- £3,400 • Solaris Antiques

Corner Cupboard

- *1800*

A fine George III one-piece standing corner cupboard in faded mahogany, the upper section having 18 panel octagonal doors. The lower section has a central drawer above two panelled moulded doors.

- *218cm x 110cm*
- **£14,500** • **M. W. & H. L.**

English Oak Dresser

- *1780*

An English oak dresser with moulded pediment and carved apron front, having four drawers on turned legs.

- *200cm x 206cm*
- **£6,950** • **Red Lion**

Expert Tips

Floor-standing corner cupboards are quite rare and the best combination has a glazed top with mid- to lower drawers and cupboards underneath.

Oak Dresser Base

- *1770*

An English oak dresser with carved fretwork, two shelves above a dresser base with three drawers, a carved apron, raised on cabriole legs with brass fittings.

- *height 95cm*
- **£8,950** • **Red Lion**

French Fruitwood Dresser

- ***18th century***

A French fruitwood dresser, with cavetto-style pediment and four shelves with carved frieze flanked by two small cupboards, with three cupboards below with decorative scrolled panelling.

- *226cm x 208cm x 54cm*
- **£5,250** • **Tredantiques**

English Cupboard

- *1700*

An English court cupboard with carved oak panels, and turned columns below a moulded pediment.

- *203cm x 150cm*
- **£3,850** • **Red Lion**

Irish Dresser

- *1780*

An Irish chestnut dresser with moulded pediment, scrolled pilasters and moulded cupboard doors.

- *200cm x 145cm*
- **£3,950** • **Red Lion**

Dumb Waiters & Whatnots

Three-Tier Stand

- ***1890***

A three-tier mahogany cake stand with fruitwood banding

- *height 89cm*
- **£195** • **Great Grooms**

Victorian Cake Stand

- ***1890***

A Victorian mahogany three-tiered cake stand with fruitwood banding.

- *height 95cm*
- **£280** • **John Clay**

Butler's Tray

- ***1850–70***

A Victorian mahogany butler's tray resting on a Georgian-style stand.

- *54cm x 65.5cm*
- **£795** • **Great Grooms**

Rosewood Cake Stand

- ***circa 1880***

Rosewood circular cake stand with a turned base.

- *height 19cm*
- **£400** • **Sign of the Times**

Mahogany Cake Stand

- ***circa 1890***

A Victorian three-tier mahogany cake stand.

- *height 87cm*
- **£195** • **Great Grooms**

Rosewood Whatnot

- ***1825***

A rosewood four-tier whatnot with small baluster turnings. Single drawer to the lower shelf, on original brass castors.

- *125cm x 46cm x 41cm*
- **£5,250** • **M. W. & H. L.**

Wall Shelves

- ***circa 1840***

A hanging wall shelf with ormolu decorative mounts made from kingswood.

- *59cm x 39cm x 15cm*
- **£1,650** • **Butchoff**

Mahogany Dumb Waiter ▲

- *circa 1850*

Three-tier mahogany dumb waiter supported by reeded columns and set on brass castors.

- *height 1.22m*
- £2,190 • **Frederick Beck**

French Tea Table ▲

- *circa 1885*

French two-tier tea table japanned on maple wood with bronze carrying handles.

- *height 83cm*
- £3,500 • **R. Hamilton**

Pot Cupboard ▼

- ***William IV***

Unusual flamed mahogany pot cupboard.

- *height 82cm*
- £850 • **V. Harvey**

Mahogany Buffet ▼

- *circa 1850*

A mid-19th-century English three-tiered buffet or dumb waiter, in mahogany, with turned supports. Each tier has a gallery and the whole is supported on original ceramic castors with brass brackets. There are two shallow drawers to the base, with carved button handles, and carved acorn finials to the top.

- *height 1.2m*
- £1,800 • **Judy Fox**

Book Etagère ▲

- *circa 1820*

An Anglo-Indian book étagère in coromandel wood with two base drawers and three shelves.

- *height 1.21m*
- £7,250 • **R. Hamilton**

Dumb Waiter ▲

- *18th century*

All mahogany with folding tiers. Turned column on a tripod base with drop levers.

- *height 1.08m*
- £3,850 • **Chambers**

Expert Tips

As the whatnot changed in function, it changed in appearance. The invention of the wood-carving machine in 1845 led to elaborate decoration for very little money.

Lowboys

Victorian Lowboy
- *circa 1900*

Walnut lowboy on cabriole legs with acanthus-leaf motif.
- *height 77cm*
- **£1,295** • **Antique Warehouse**

Expert Tips

Lowboys were sometimes made in solid wood, particularly oak, and sometimes with straight legs. The most sought after, however, are those that are veneered and on cabriole legs.

Reproduction Lowboy
- *circa 1930*

Reproduction of a four-drawer, 18th-century, walnut lowboy, with crossbanded marquetry and raised on cabriole legs with pad feet.
- *height 75cm*
- **£395** • **Fulham**

Mahogany Lowboy
- *circa 1740*

An 18th-century, Chippendale-period, well-figured mahogany lowboy with three drawers, two small below one large, with original brass mounts, the whole raised on cabriole legs with pad feet. The piece has an unusually shaped kneehole and apron, reflecting its original purpose as a dressing-table.
- *height 71cm*
- **£3,500** • **L. & E. Kreckovic**

Dutch Lowboy
- *circa 1750*

A fine, Dutch, 18th-century lowboy, with serpentine front and quarter drawers each side of the two main drawers. Original handles and fine marquetry decoration.
- *height 77cm*
- **£8,250** • **Chambers**

George I Lowboy
- *circa 1720*

A fine George I lowboy in figured walnut, with three drawers with original mounts.
- *height 72.5cm*
- **£40,000** • **Norman Adams**

Regency Lowboy
- *circa 1820*

An English 19th-century lowboy, in walnut, with three drawers and brass mounts, the whole on cabriole legs.
- *height 72cms*
- **£2,700** • **Mora &Upham**

Mirrors

Overmantel Mirrors

- ***circa 1850s***

One of a pair of Victorian moulded giltwood overmantel mirrors.

- *128cm x 65cm*
- £1,950 • **Old Cinema**

Queen Anne Mirror

- ***circa 1710***

Rare black lacquer Queen Anne table mirror of large proportions, retaining the original glass with bureau front on turned bun feet.

- *95cm x 48cm*
- £4,900 • **Ashcombe House**

Brass Mirror

- ***1800***

A brass circular mirror with foliate designs and two candlestick holders attached to a pierced metal back.

- *26cm x 42cm*
- £350 • **New Century**

Oak-Framed Mirror

- ***19th century***

An English carved oak mirror, with ogee moulding above a dentil course and carved frieze, the mirror flanked by turned pillars.

- *120cm x 90cm*
- £480 • **Old Cinema**

Expert Tips

The dressing table or table mirror reached its zenith in the Queen Anne period.

Gilded Overmantel Mirror

- ***circa 1860s***

A Victorian overmantel mirror with serpentine arch and a gilded, moulded edge

- *130cm x 64cm*
- £850 • **Old Cinema**

Mahogany Table Mirror

- ***1780***

George III mahogany serpentine fronted mirror on ogee moulded feet with original patination.

- *height 58cm*
- £1,550 • **Ashcombe House**

Venetian Mirror

- *circa 1890*

A highly ornate, oval Venetian etched-crest mirror.

- *height 1.32m*
- £2,850
- Through the Looking Glass

Venetian Mirror

- *circa 1850*

A fine etched and engraved Venetian mirror.

- *height 148cm*
- £3,300 • Paul Andrews

Expert Tips

Test for the use of stucco with a needle on the reverse of the frame. It will penetrate wood but not stucco.

Trumeau Mirror

- *circa 1885*

A slim, gilt continental trumeau mirror, showing pastoral scene.

- *height 123cm*
- £1,600
- Through the Looking Glass

Toilet Mirror

- *circa 1780*

A Chinese export lacquered toilet mirror.

- *height 68cm*
- £3,850 • P.L. James

Italian Mirror

- *circa 1890*

Small, rectangular giltwood and fretted Florentine mirror.

- *height 55cm*
- £850
- Through the Looking Glass

Victorian Gilt Mirror

- *circa 1890*

Gilt mirror with shelf scrolls hatch, broken pediment and heart-shaped mirror.

- *height 100cm*
- £850
- Through the Looking Glass

Toilet Mirror

- *circa 1760*

An unusual Chippendale-period carved mahogany toilet mirror.

- *height 60cm*
- £15,000 • Norman Adams

Regency Mirror

- *circa 1830*

A Regency gilt mirror, decorated with balls, vine églomisé and with Corinthian columns.

- *height 82.5cm*
- **£1,350**
- **Through the Looking Glass**

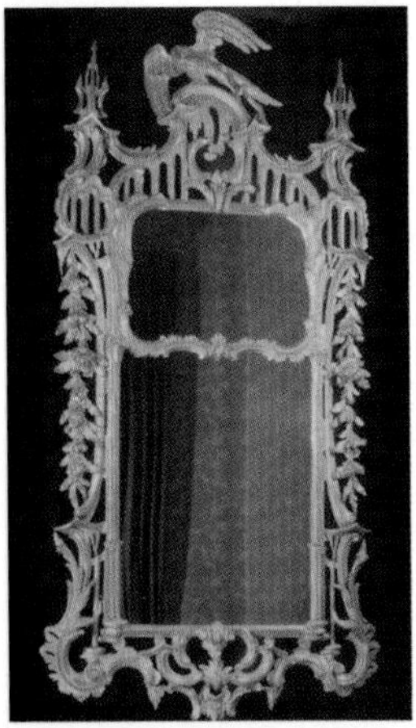

Chippendale Mirror

- *circa 1760*

A fine Chippendale-period gilded, carved-wood mirror.

- *height 2.32m*
- **£125,000** • **Norman Adams**

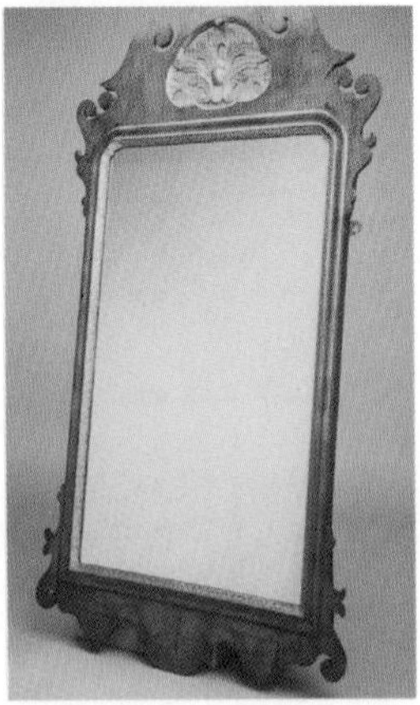

George II Wall Mirror

- *circa 1760*

A walnut, fret-cut mirror with gilded motif and inner slip.

- *height 91.5cm*
- **£875** • **J. Collins**

English Mirror

- *circa 1890*

An English carved giltwood mandolin and flute top mirror.

- *height 72.5cm*
- **£650**
- **Through the Looking Glass**

Regency Dressing Mirror

- *circa 1820*

A mahogany dressing mirror with three drawers outlined with boxwood stringing.

- *height 65cm*
- **£950** • **J. Collins**

George III Mirror

- *circa 1770*

A good, oval Chippendale mirror.

- *height 1.33m*
- **£16,500** • **P.L. James**

Console and Mirror

- *circa 1830*

A mahogany console and mirror, with architectural pillars supporting the pediment.

- *height 250cm*
- **£4,850** • **Ranby Hall**

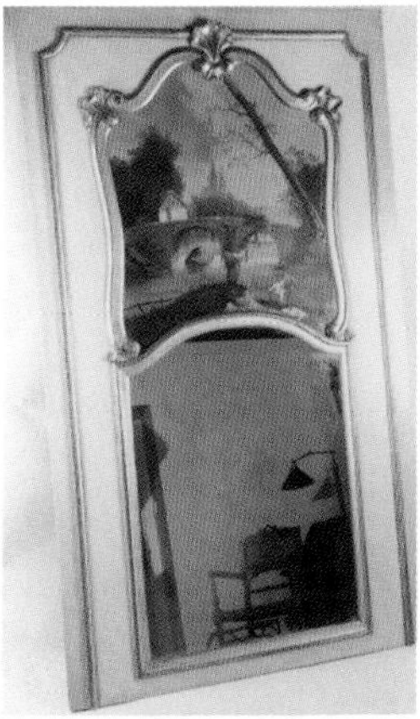

French Mirror
- ***19th century***

A French mirror with painted panel and gilt moulded shell and scrolling decoration.
- *height 170cm*
- £2,200 • **Lynda Franklin**

Venetian Mirror
- ***circa 1850***

An etched and engraved Venetian mirror.
- *height 150cm*
- £3,700 • **Paul Andrews**

Expert Tips

To check the thickness, and thus the approximate age, of mirror glass, place a pencil, or other pointed object, on to the glass and judge the distance between the point and its image.

Chippendale Mirror
- ***circa 1770***

A small Chippendale-period mirror, carved and gilded.
- *height 90cm*
- £6,200 • **P.L. James**

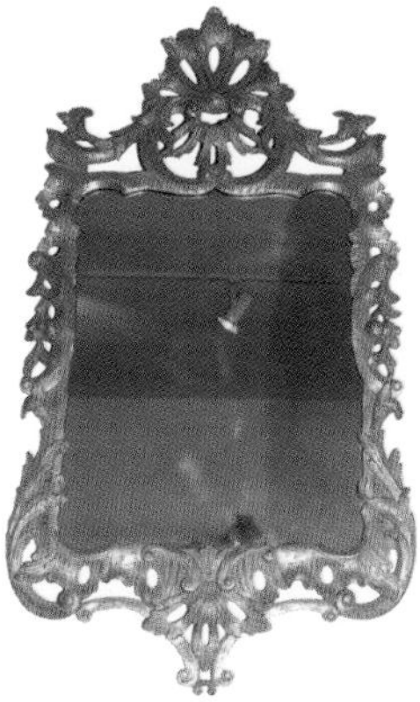

Chippendale Mirror
- ***circa 1760***

A small, cartouche-shaped, carved wood and gilt mirror.
- *height 89cm*
- £8,000 • **Norman Adams**

Lacquered Toilet Mirror
- ***circa 1790***

Chinese export-lacquered toilet mirror on four-drawer pedestal.
- *height 68cm*
- £3,850 • **P.L. James**

Skeleton Dressing Mirror
- ***circa 1825***

A dressing mirror, in mahogany, with Dutch-drop side screws and acorn finials.
- *height 61cm*
- £475 • **J. Collins**

Adam-Manner Mirror
- ***circa 1875***

Adam-manner neo-classical urn and husks on a oval gilt mirror.
- *height 85cm*
- £1,350
- **Through the Looking Glass**

Walnut Wall Mirror

- ***circa 1920s***

George II-style walnut and parcel-gilt wall mirror with swan neck pediment and beaded edges.

- *112cm x 68cm*
- **£1,250** • **M. Luther**

English Regency Mirror

- ***circa 1810***

An English regency convex giltwood mirror, surmounted with a carved eagle.

- *112cm x 76cm*
- **£5,400** • **M. Luther**

Hour-Glass Mirror

- ***1800***

A giltwood hour-glass-shaped mirror surmounted by an urn with trailing foliage, with two candelabra, with cut glass droplets.

- *96cm x 46cm*
- **£9,500** • **O.F. Wilson**

Lacquered Hall Mirror

- ***19th century***

A lacquered oak-framed hall mirror with moulded edge.

- *122cm x 48cm*
- **£2,850** • **M. Luther**

Oval Wall Mirror

- ***19th century***

Nineteenth-century English giltwood oval wall mirror with carved floral decoration.

- *130cm x 111cm*
- **£4,950** • **M. Luther**

Giltwood Wall Mirror

- ***circa 1880***

A George I-style giltwood wall mirror with a carved mask decoration.

- *122cm x 81cm*
- **£3,200** • **M. Luther**

Regency Mirror

- ***1830***

A Regency wall mirror with a carved frieze depicting shepherds and their flock within architectural details.

- *height 57cm*
- **£2,350** • **Ashcombe House**

Oval Gilt Mirror

- ***1895***

Victorian oval gilt mirror with a carved moulded border.

- *height 125cm*
- **£1,400** • **Looking Glass**

Expert Tips

The convex mirror rose to fame in the public eye when seen in the painting The Marriage *by Vermeer. The convex mirror, like a fish eye lens, has the ability to capture the whole room within its frame.*

Swedish Mirror

- ***circa 1860***

Ninteenth-century giltwood and painted overmantel mirror with original finish, after a neo-classical style.

- *178cm x 170cm*
- **£6,900** • **M. Luther**

Regency Mirror

- ***1820***

Regency convex gilt mirror surmounted with an eagle and decorated with carved acanthus leaf and beading.

- *117cm x 64cm*
- **£3,680** • **Looking Glass**

George III Mirror

- ***1800***

A George III carved wood mirror with water gilding in a chinoiserie style.

- *134cm x 82cm*
- **£3,300** • **Looking Glass**

Octagonal Mirror

- ***circa 1850***

French cushion gilt with reverse shell base and profuse flowers.

- *height 132cm*
- **£2,500**
- **Through the Looking Glass**

Wall Mirror

- ***Early 18th century***

An unusual early eighteenth-century wall mirror.

- *100cm x 80cm*
- **£4,800** • **M. Luther**

Miscellaneous

Blackamoor Torchères

- *mid-19th century*

Fruitwood torchères with serpentine tops, figures and acanthus-leaf body on tripod base.

- *height 91cm*
- £2,850 • **Lesley Bragge**

Library Steps

- *circa 1900*

Oak library steps with carved decoration to the sides.

- *height 47cm*
- £500 • **Lacquer Chest**

Painted Jardinière

- *late 19th century*

Painted steel body with floral scrolled handles.

- *height 21cm*
- £90 • **Riverbank**

Corner Washstand

- *circa 1800*

Mahogany, two-drawer washstand, the top with a rounded splashback.

- *height 86.5cm*
- £1,250 • **J. Collins**

Cane Jardinière

- *late 19th century*

Gilt, cane top with leaf decoration and cloven feet.

- *height 101cm*
- £550 • **Youlls**

Birdcage

- *circa 1940*

A 20th-century birdcage of rectangular shape with covered back and sides.

- *height 31cm*
- £22 • **Curios**

Regency Bookcarrier

- *circa 1810*

A fine Regency bookcarrier in the Bullock style with a drawer below.

- *width 43cm*
- £2,350 • **P.L. James**

Plate Drainer

• *circa 1910*
A pine draining board for drying dishes, with carved ends.
• *width 64cm*
• £150 • Lacquer Chest

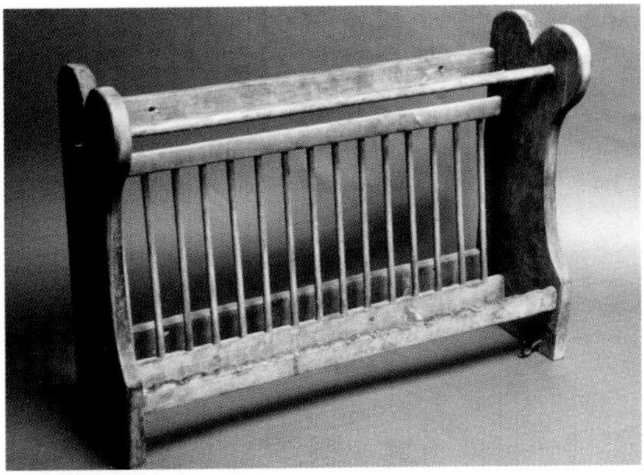

Wine Cooler

• *circa 1810*
Regency mahogany wine cooler of oval form, with brass inlay.
• *height 55.5cm*
• £18,000 • Norman Adams

Regency Jardinière

• *circa 1820*
A Regency painted metal jardinière of octagonal form with chinoiserie designs.
• *length 41.5cm*
• £3,250 • O.F. Wilson

Mahogany Washstand

• *circa 1860*
Washstand with recesses for wash bowls, with good patination.
• *height 99cm*
• £780 • Ranby Hall

Mahogany Cellaret

• *circa 1790*
A mahogany cellaret with boxwood stringing and chequered line inlay.
• *height 66cm*
• £3,250 • J. de Haan

Mahogany Torchère

• *19th century*
With inlay on a long fluted pedestal with a tripod base.
• *height 148cm*
• £390 • Youlls

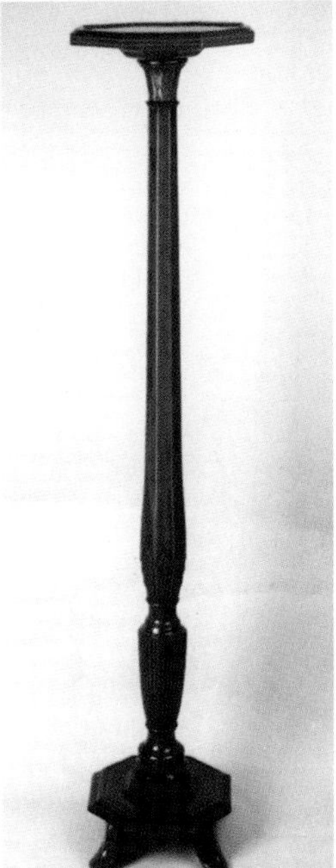

Shop Drawers

• *circa 1880*
Mahogany shop-drawer cabinet with twelve drawers.
• *height 90cm*
• £495 • Lacquer Chest

Gothic Hall Stand

- ***late 19th century***

French hall stand with profusely carved tracery and lifting seat.

- *height 242cm*
- **£1,400** • **Youlls**

Georgian Whatnot

- ***circa 1780***

A Georgian, mahogany, four-shelved whatnot.

- *height 138m*
- **£2,500** • **Terence Morse**

Waste Paper Baskets

- ***circa 1910***

Silver plated. With pierced rim and frieze of rabbits below.

- *height 33cm*
- **£880** • **Lesley Bragge**

Victorian Bucket

- ***circa 1860***

Oak bucket with brass hoops, silver wash, brass handle and name plaque.

- *height 33cm*
- **£150** • **Albany**

Towel Rail

- ***19th century***

A good quality mahogany Victorian towel rail with turned decoration.

- *height 95cm*
- **£265** • **Old Cinema**

Open Wine Cooler

- ***circa 1775***

An Adam-period wine cooler with ram's head handles.

- *height 49.5cm*
- **£17,500** • **Norman Adams**

Ebonised Pedestal

- ***19th century***

Nineteenth century ebonised pedestal in the form of a griffin.

- *height 111cm*
- **£2,850** • **S. Duggan**

George III Bucket

- *circa 1790*

A mahogany brass-bound bucket of navette shape.

- *height 33cm*
- £2,350 • J. de Haan

Lacquered Stand

- *late 19th century*

Stand with mirror and brass candleholders, lacquered with mother-of-pearl and gilt floral decoration.

- *height 125cm*
- £950 • Lynda Franklin

Whip and Boot Stand

- *circa 1830*

A whip and boot stand in fruitwood with finial tops.

- *height 94cm*
- £450 • Castlegate

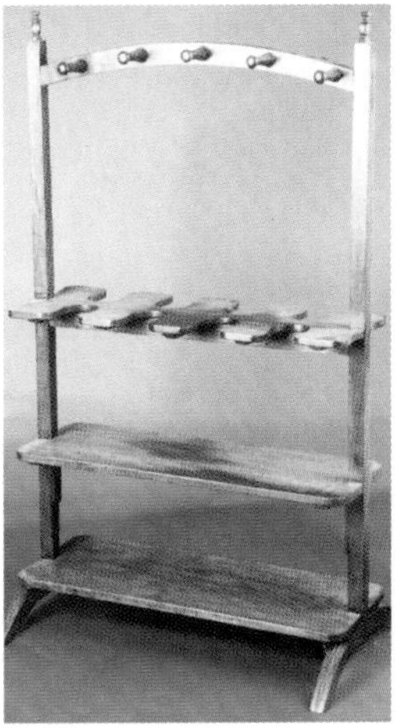

Pair of Knife Boxes

- *circa 1890*

Inlaid mahogany with stepped interiors, marquetry decoration and boxwood stringing.

- *height 68cm (closed)*
- £9,000 • Judy Fox

Teak Trolley

- *circa 1880*

A three-shelved teak trolley with two large, spoked wheels.

- *height 100cm*
- £300 • Lacquer Chest

Four Tier Whatnot

- *circa 1825*

A mahogany "plum pudding" veneered whatnot with a one-piece top and an oak-lined drawer.

- *height 131cm*
- £3,250 • J. Collins

Oval Tea Tray

- *circa 1790*

A tray of the Sheraton period, having a wavy edge with the outside inlaid with joined loops.

- *width 71cm*
- £850 • J. Collins

Mahogany Shaving Stand ❮

- *circa 1880*

An English mahogany shaving stand with circular mirror on a carved and turned tripod base with drop finial.

- *height 135cm*
- £685 • Tredantiques

Georgian Wash Stand ❯

- *1820*

A George III wash stand with hinged top enclosing basin above a sliding door on tapered legs.

- *height 75cm x 40cm*
- £1,800 • C.H. Major

Oak Stand ▲

- *circa 1780*

A charming and rare eighteenth century oak stand, on tripod base with splayed feet.

- *height 72cm*
- £1,450 • Rod Wilson

Indian Shrine ❮

- *late 18th century*

An Indian Hindu shrine with pink moulded dome with pierced iron rail, ornately decorated with carved pillars painted pink and green, standing on a square base.

- *153cm x 76cm x 76cm*
- £4,700 • Gordon Reece

Rice Bucket ❯

- *1880*

Chinese rice bucket with brass fittings, central carved handle and painted Chinese characters.

- *31cm x 25cm*
- £50 • Great Grooms

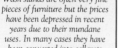

Expert Tips

Wash stands are often very fine pieces of furniture but the prices have been depressed in recent years due to their mundane uses. In many cases they have been converted into cellarets and hi fi cabinets but are now becoming accepted pieces in their own right.

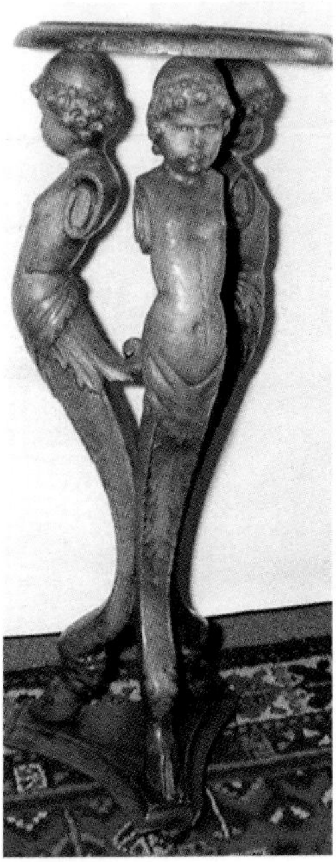

Cast-Iron Victorian Hall Stand

- *1880*

Cast-iron Victorian hall stand with gilding, marble top and gothic tracery.

- *200cm x 65cm x 30cm*
- £1,250 • **Tredantique**

Pair of Jardinières

- *circa 1840*

A pair of walnut tripod jardinières with scrolled feet and original copper lines.

- *height 107cm*
- £14,500 • **M. W. & H. L.**

Jardinière Stand

- *1780*

A walnut jardinière stand on a tripod base carved as cherubs, with cloven feet.

- *height 79cm*
- £1,400 • **Sign of the Times**

Coal Box in Sarcophagus Form

- *1890*

A nineteenth-century mahogany coal box in sarcophagus form with lid and a brass handle.

- *54cm x 33cm*
- £395 • **Great Grooms**

Umbrella and Coat Stand

- *circa 1790*

In patinated mahogany with fine shaped pegs and turned finials. With original zinc liner.

- *height 181cm*
- £2,850 • **M. W. & H. L.**

Expert Tips

In the last ten years, ornate and finely executed umbrella and coat stands have become extremely expensive, and increasingly desirable, with the finer examples employing gothic tracery and fantastical designs. The humble coat stand has established its place as a highly attractive piece of furniture that has a constant usage in our daily lives.

Screens

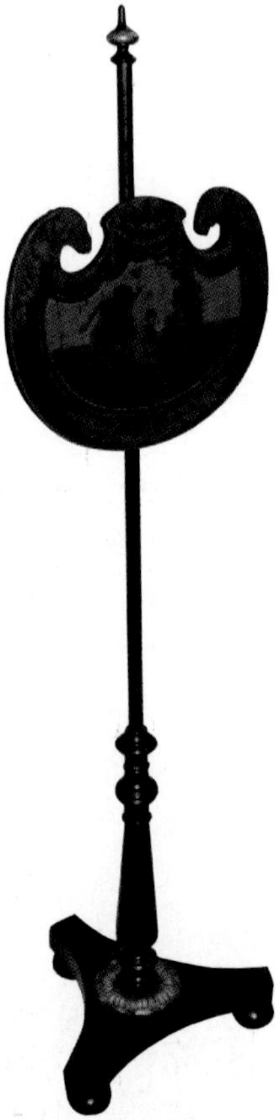

Ebonised Fire Screen

- *1820*

A Regency ebonised fire screen, in the shape of a shield on a tapered stand with tripod base and bun feet.

- *135cm x 38cm*
- £650 • **Mac Humble**

Mahogany Pole Screen

- *1830–37*

A William IV mahogany pole screen with a tapestry of golden pheasant in petit point.

- *height 153cm*
- £975 • **Harpur Deardren**

Georgian Screen

- *circa 1840*

A Georgian screen with sliding side screens and turned stretchers.

- *90cm x 40cm*
- £695 • **Sign of the Times**

Expert Tips

The pole screen was an adjustable version of the screen that could be used to protect the makeup and complexion of the sitter from the heat of the fire. Larger panelled screens were devised as a decorative means of ensuring privacy as well as a method of draught exclusion.

Regency Fire Screen

- *1820*

Regency mahogany fire screen with brass urn finials.

- *94cm x 57cm*
- £1,200 • **Sign of the Times**

Chinese Screen

- *1850*

One of a pair of antique Chinese filigree screens with geometric designs made of cypress wood.

- *109cm x 51cm*
- £1,350 • **Gordon Reece**

Settees & Sofas

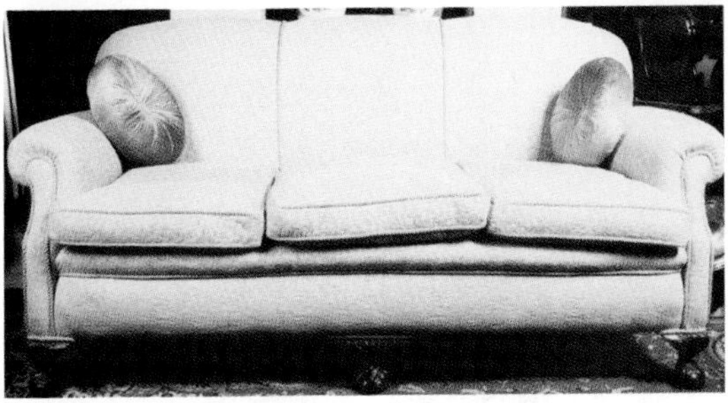

Wing Sofa ❮

- *circa 1880*

Armchair sofa raised upon ebonised cabriole legs on padded feet.

- *height 1.3m*
- £1,850 • **Ranby Hall**

Canopy Sofa ❮

- *circa 1880*

An unusual ebonised cherry wood and canopy sofa. Bow-backed tortiene carvings and lovely scroll shape overall.

- *width 1.95m*
- £2,800 • **Sieff**

Regency Window Seat ▲

- *circa 1820*

English Regency cane window seat with original gilding and polychrome paints.

- *width 1.52m*
- £3,700 • **Mora & Upham**

Cane Sofa ❯

- *19th century*

Cane sofa and two chairs, with studded upholstery backs and tunnel and fluted legs.

- *width 1.4m*
- £3,400 • **L. Franklin**

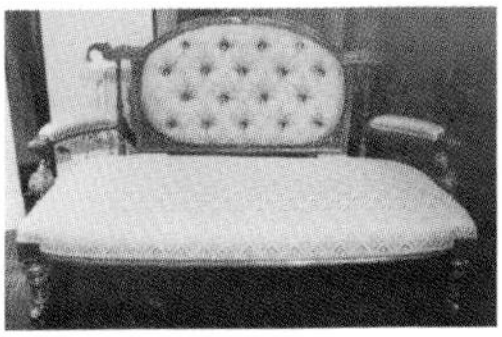

Victorian Sofa ▲

- *circa 1870*

Walnut sofa on turned legs with carved arm rests.

- *width 1.53m*
- £2,900 • **L. & E. Kreckovic**

Victorian Sofa ❯

- *circa 1820*

Howard-style cream-coloured sofa, complete in selling fabric, raised on terracotta castors with brass fittings.

- *width 1.5m*
- £1,450 • **Tredantiques**

Country House Settee ❮

- *circa 1810*

English painted rosewood settee in the George Smith manner. On castors with fleur de lys design.

- *width 2.09m*
- £4,800
- **M. Luther & P. Goodwin**

Gustavian Suite

• *circa 1880*
Suite of Gustavian-style furniture including a sofa, pair of armchairs and four chairs.
• **£5,600 (suite)** • **Cavendish**

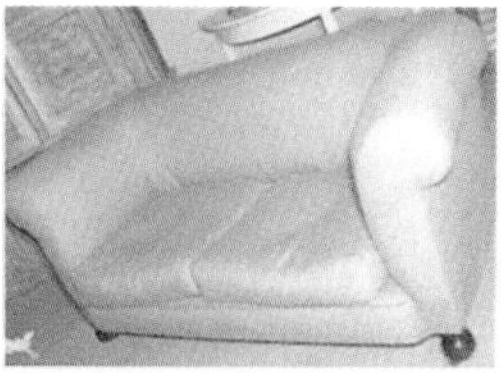

Chesterfield Sofa

• *circa 1900*
A two-seater chesterfield with mahogany bun feet and brass castors, covered in hessian.
• *width 1.72m*
• **£1,250** • **Annette Puttnam**

Leather Sofa

• *circa 1840*
A 19th-century, two-seater upholstered sofa, in original black leather, with brass castors and mahogany legs.
• *width 2.06m*
• **£3,600** • **D. Martin-Taylor**

Three-Seater Sofa

• *19th century*
Upholstery and cushions in good condition.
• *width 1.92m*
• **£1,850** • **Ranby Hall**

Sofa & Two Chairs

• *circa 1860*
A red silk sofa with two chairs. Gilt decoration to frame.
• *width 1.62m (sofa)*
• *width 64cm (chairs)*
• **£1,200 (all)**
• **Mora & Upham**

Silk Sofa

• *circa 1860*
A beige and gold silk-covered sofa with gilt decoration.
• *width 1.2m*
• **£2,200** • **Mora & Upham**

Regency Settee

• *1830*
A Regency mahogany classical style settee with a serpentine apron front with curved back and scroll ends, and curved cornucopaiae style legs terminating in foliate castors.
• *width 2.1m*
• **£3,650** • **Ranby Hall**

George III Settee

• *circa 1890*

A George III-style mahogany settee, with shaped back and scrolled arm rests on chamfered legs.

• *78cm x 175cm x 60cm*

• **£1,850** • **Ranby Hall**

French Restoration Sofa

• *1820*

French Restoration-period sofa with a moulded wood frame painted cream with gilt banding, on stylised bun feet, designed by Julian Chichester.

• *81cm x 202cm x 78cm*

• **£3,800** • **Ranby Hall**

Birchwood Sofa

• *circa 1890*

Swedish birchwood Biedermeier style sofa with ebonised, architecturally styled arms.

• *97cm x 211cm x 75cm*

• **£4,900** • **Rupert Cavendish**

Double-Ended Mahogany Sofa

• *early 19th century*

An early nineteenth-century mahogany double-ended sofa. Upholstered in selling fabric.

• *152cm x 205cm x 65cm*

• **£3,995** • **Harpur Deardren**

French Giltwood Sofa

• *circa 1860*

A giltwood French Louis XV-style canapé with curved, arched padded back and sides and a serpentine apron on cabriole legs.

• *120cm x 120cm x 69cm*

• **£6,800** • **Ranby Hall**

Biedermeier Sofa

• *circa 1860*

A Biedermeier mahogany sofa with lyre back and scrolled shaped arms with carved bun feet.

• *106cm x 274cm x 64cm*

• **£5,600** • **Ranby Hall**

Stools

Chippendale-Style Stool

- *Victorian*

Late Victorian stool in the Chippendale style on ball and claw feet.

- *40cm x 47cm x 34cm*
- **£425** • **Fay Orton**

Louis XV Stool

- ***circa 1760***

A Louis XV walnut stool with a circular buttoned top, the seat rail scrolled to meet the cabriole legs standing on a whirl foot with a scrolled stretcher.

- *height 75cm*
- **£1,650** • **Butchoff**

French Giltwood Stool

- ***circa 1811***

A Louis XVI giltwood stool with moulded frame and floral carving standing on cabriole legs.

- *46cm x 38cm x 86cm*
- **£2,200** • **O.F. Wilson**

Carved Mahogany Stool

- *1835*

A finely carved mahogany stool of good design and colour. Flowing X-frame legs with stretcher supports.

- *48cm x 69cm x 38cm*
- **£2,950** • **Mac Humble**

Painted Tabourets

- *1790*

Pair of late eighteenth century tabourets with painted decoration. Fluted tapered legs and carved frieze.

- *16cm x 31cm x 25cm*
- **£2,600** • **O.F. Wilson**

Queen Anne Stool

- ***1710***

A rare Queen Anne period stool in walnut circular top mounted on four carved cabriole legs with turned stretcher.

- *height 47cm*
- **£15,500** • **M. W. & H. L.**

Expert Tips

A set of two or more stools is rare and can considerably enhance the price.

Pair Of Empire Stools

• ***circa* 1820**
A pair of Swedish stools designed by the architect Sundvall.
• *height 42cm*
• £2,700 • **Cavendish**

Cane Stool

• ***circa* 1900**
An Edwardian Louis XV-style gilt and caned stool on cabriole legs with scrolled feet.
• *height 42cm*
• £295 • **French Room**

French Stool

• ***circa* 1820**
French mahogany "X"-frame stool with upholstered top.
• *length 52cm*
• £685 • **M. J. Bowdery**

Pouffe Sculpte Stool

• ***19th century***
Walnut *pouffe sculpte rectangulaire* stool, with shell motif, resting on cabriole legs.
• *height 60cm*
• £950 • **Lynda Franklin**

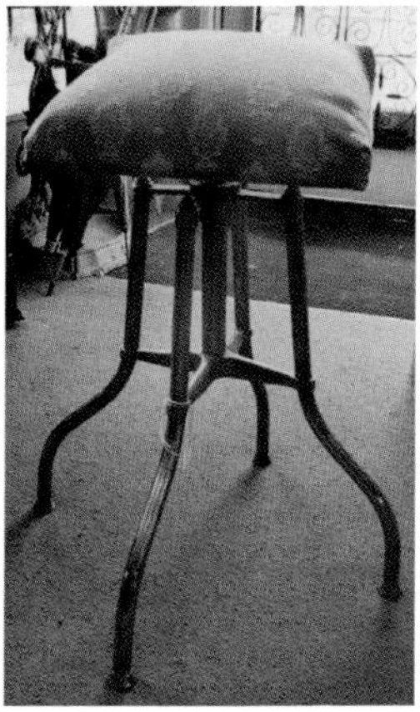

Brass Stool

• ***circa* 1910**
Edwardian brass piano stool of adjustable height with red fabric.
• *height 90cm*
• £175 • **Fulham**

Expert Tips

When examining a stool, check for hessian under the seat. Hessian was never used before 1840 – and it is often used to conceal an alteration.

Oak Stepstool

• ***circa* 1880**
A 19th-century oak, three-stepped stepstool.
• *height 70cm*
• £290 • **Lacquer Chest**

Leather Stool

• ***19th century***
Victorian rosewood stool with leather button upholstery on claw and ball feet.
• *length 1.4m*
• £1,800 • **Old Cinema**

Mahogany Stools

• 1880
A pair of Hepplewhite mahogany stools with scrolled arms, padded seats and standing on tapered legs.
• *73cm x 66cm*
• £2,650 • **J. Fox**

Giltwood Stools

• 1880
A pair of French Louis VXI giltwood stools with scrolled arms on cabriole legs.
• *50cm x 75cm x 52cm*
• £2,850 • **J. Fox**

Piano Stool

• 1890
Victorian piano stool with green leather seat on carved acanthus leaf legs.
• *height 51cm*
• £400 • **J. Fox**

Expert Tips

Stools come in many shapes, sizes and dimensions and remain extremely popular among collectors. Here again, look out for the Victorian and twentieth-century copies of period pieces.

Pair of Walnut Stools

• 1870
A pair of Victorian walnut stools, on bulbous turned legs.
• *18cm x 35cm*
• £650 • **J. Fox**

Biedermeier Bench

• circa 1820
North German Biedermeier bench. Birchwood and masur birch.
• *50cm x 94cm x 68cm*
• £3,400 • **R. Cavendish**

Expert Tips

Piano stools are always popular but their adjustment mechanisms must be studied closely, especially the cabriole leg version, as in some cases these have been exposed to extreme pressure and are weakened or damaged. Walnut versions should be closely checked for woodworm.

Tables

Pair of Tables

- ***circa* 1890**

A pair of Regency-style, continental, gilded and painted console tables, with rich, ornate carving and variegated marble.

- *height 92cm*
- **£18,500 • Rupert Cavendish**

Urn Table

- ***circa* 1760**

An unusual Chippendale-period mahogany urn table, with fret gallery, inlaid floral side panels and turned, fluted legs.

- *height 61cm*
- **£33,000 • Norman Adams**

Swedish Sofa Table

- ***circa* 1915**

Swedish sofa table in birchwood, with central, ebonised column, folding side flaps and a central drawer.

- *length (flaps up) 90cm*
- **£3,900 • Rupert Cavendish**

Marquetry Table

- ***circa* 1850**

19th-century French marquetry table with floral designs and brass mounts.

- *height 71cm*
- **£1,250 • Lynda Franklin**

Tripod Table

- ***circa* 1820**

A solid, circular mahogany tripod table with one-piece tilt top raised on a well-turned support.

- *height 75cm*
- **£1,650 • J. Collins**

French Side Table

- ***19th century***

French painted side table with marble inset top and caned platforms on turned and fluted legs with floral swags.

- *height 75cm*
- **£700 • Youlls Antiques**

Card Table

- ***circa* 1880**

French card table, cross-banded with floral marquetry and stringing. Has brass moulding, ormolu mounts and original baize.

- *height 75cm*
- **£3,100 • Lesley Bragge**

Expert Tips

Carved marine subject motifs, such as dolphins, anchors, tridents and others, were used as a tribute to the victories of Horatio Nelson. Items with such carvings on them, therefore, are unlikely to pre-date 1800.

Inlaid Regency Tables

- *circa 1810*

A pair of Regency polescreens converted into tables.

- *height 80cm*
- £3,250 • P.L. James

French Side Table

- *circa 1880*

Painted French side table with marble top and rosette decoration on turned and fluted legs.

- *height 79cm*
- £350 • Youlls Antiques

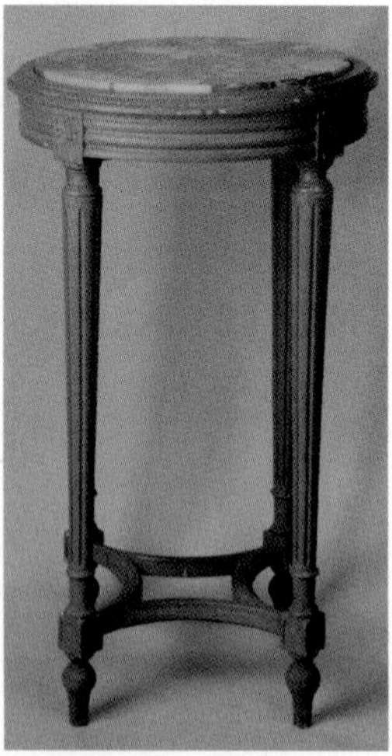

Dining Table

- *circa 1810*

Mahogany D-ended Regency dining table, cross-banded in kingwood with boxwood stringing.

- *length (fully extended) 195cm*
- £8,750 • J. Collins

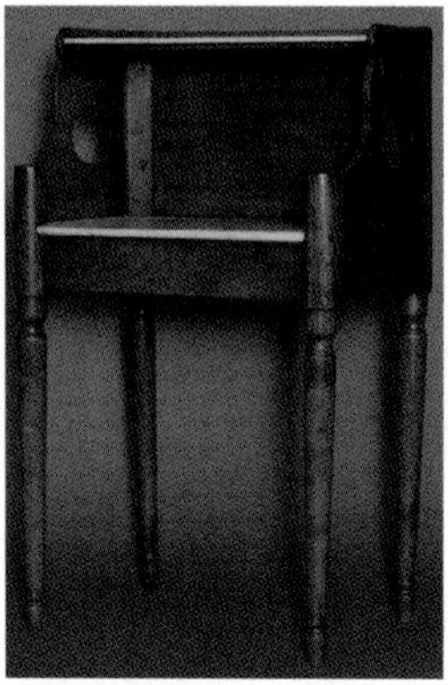

Table de Chevet

- *circa 1790*

Table de chevet in cherrywood with marble shelves.

- *height 72cm*
- £2,200 • O.F. Wilson

Supper Table

- *circa 1780*

Georgian mahogany tambour-fronted gentleman's supper table on square legs with side flaps.

- *height 70cm*
- £4,000 • Castlegate

Painted Side Table

- *circa 1860*

Painted side table of oval form with inset marble top, set on turned, fluted legs. Oval cupboard at base with oval cane panel.

- *height 75cm*
- £650 • Youlls Antiques

Gueridon Table

- *circa 1830*

A very good gueridon French table, with an unusual marble top and acanthus scroll legs.

- *height 71cm*
- £6,750 • Christopher Preston

Gateleg Table

• ***circa 1740***

A fine George II almost circular walnut table.

• *height 72cm*

• **£40,000** • **Norman Adams**

Pier Table

• ***circa 1820***

Regency pier table with fluted column supports and pleated panel to rear.

• *height 103cm*

• **£1,895** • **M.J. Bowdery**

Mahogany Side Table

• ***circa 1780***

Small Georgian mahogany side table, with single drawer.

• *height 72cm*

• **£1,800** • **Terence Morse**

Snap-Top Table

• ***circa 1800***

Georgian, mahogany, snap-top occasional table with rectangular top with rounded corners and tripod base with swept feet terminating in castors.

• *height 102cm*

• **£800** • **Ian Spencer**

Elephant Table

• ***circa 1900***

Very detailed, carved table sitting on four elephants' heads, the trunks as legs, with ivory tusks.

• *height 62cm*

• **£1,250** • **Christopher Preston**

Card Table

• ***circa 1790***

George III mahogany card table.

• *height 71cm*

• **£3,950** • **J. de Haan**

Cherrywood Table

• ***circa 1760***

French table on cabriole legs.

• *length 180cm*

• **£3,200** • **Lynda Franklin**

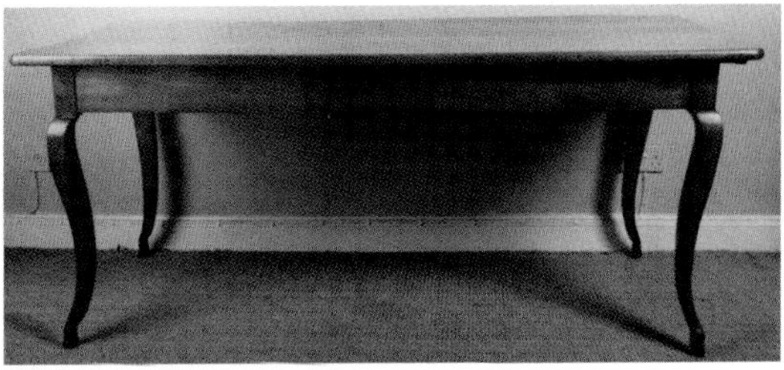

Art Deco Coffee Table

- ***circa 1925***

Swedish walnut table with inlays of heart, burr elm and fruitwood.

- *diameter 100cm*
- £2,700 • **Rupert Cavendish**

Games Table

- ***circa 1840***

Rosewood games table of exceptional quality with original ormolu paw feet.

- *height 74cm*
- £3,800 • **Ranby Hall**

Pier Table

- ***circa 1790***

A shallow Sheraton-period satinwood pier table.

- *height 86cm*
- £22,500 • **Norman Adams**

Side Table

- ***19th century***

French oval side table.

- *height 75cm*
- £650 • **Youlls Antiques**

Marble Table

- ***18th century***

French white marble table with fine bronze mounts and three columns on a tri-cornered plinth.

- *height 71cm*
- £2,700 • **Lynda Franklin**

Side Table

- ***circa 1870***

Mid-Victorian mahogany, two-drawer side table.

- *height 75cm*
- £1,850 • **Browns Antiques**

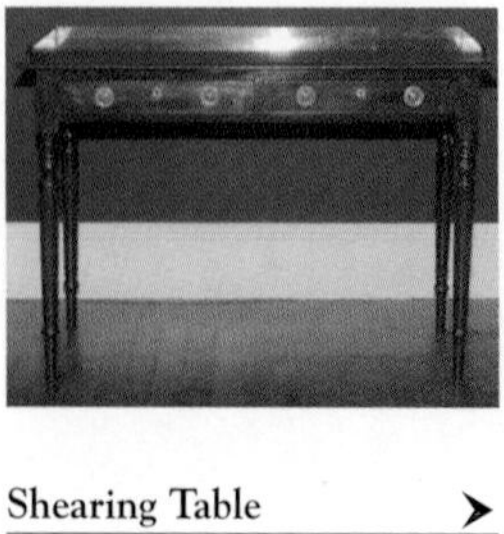

Shearing Table

- ***circa 1850***

Primitive, V-shaped wooden table for sheep-shearing.

- *height 38cm*
- £520 • **Lacquer Chest**

Sewing Table

- ***circa* 1870**

Victorian walnut writing and sewing table with leaf-decorated, turned cabriole legs and satinwood floral inlay.

- *height 73cm*
- **£1,650** • **Castlegate**

Tea Table

- ***circa* 1800**

George III mahogany tea table with line inlay.

- *height 75cm*
- **£1,745** • **M.J. Bowdery**

Games Table

- ***circa* 1835**

Mahogany, fold-over games table raised on central pedestal.

- *height 75cm*
- **£1,650** • **Ranby Hall**

Yew Tilt Table

- ***circa* 1760**

Fine 18th-century yew tilt table with tripod base.

- *height 67cm*
- **£2,250** • **Red Lion**

Side Table

- ***circa* 1690**

Exceptional William and Mary marquetry side table with "X" stretcher and original bun feet.

- *height 71cm*
- **£4,400** • **Raffety**

Expert Tips

Dryness in the atmosphere caused by central heating is furniture's greatest enemy. There are various methods of humidifying the atmosphere; using one of them is essential.

Pembroke Table

- ***circa* 1770**

English mahogany Pembroke table of typical form, veneered with satin and tulipwood, strung with ebony and boxwood. The table has drawers at either end with brass fittings, a side flap and the whole rests on four square tapering legs terminating in brass castors.

- *height 74cm*
- **£4,850**
- **M. Wakelin & H. Linfield**

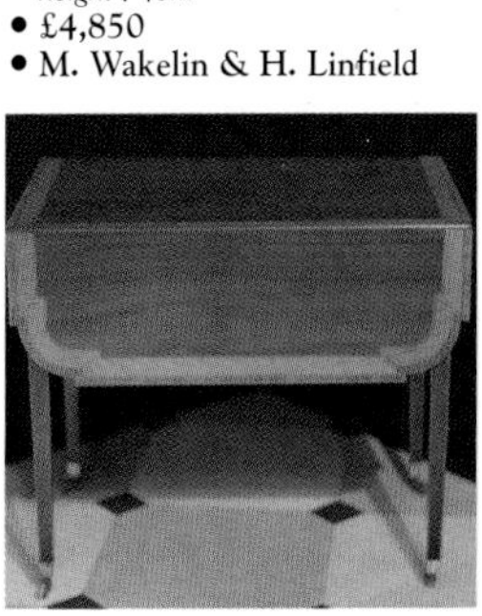

Breakfast Table

- ***circa* 1810**

Regency mahogany breakfast table with tilt top.

- *height 70cm*
- **£12,500** • **J. Collins**

Hall Table and Chairs

- ***1850***

An oak hall suite comprising a table on turned legs with carved back, and two hall chairs. Rigin style, marked "SP".

- *width 94cm (table)*
- **£3,350** • **Mac Humble**

Ebonised Table

- ***circa 1890***

Hexagonal ebonised table with green leather top, standing on four turned legs with a hoof pad foot.

- *60cm x 58cm*
- **£800** • **New Century**

Regency Table

- ***1812–1830***

Regency mahogany table on an ebonised, X-framed stretcher base.

- *71cm x 107cm*
- **£3,350** • **The Old Cinema**

Satinwood Table

- ***1815***

Satinwood table banded in rosewood, on a single pedestal on a tripod base with scrolled feet.

- *74cm x 52cm*
- **£5,900** • **Dial Post House**

Standing Tray

- ***1780***

A satinwood tray on stand, with detachable tray with brass fittings and reeded legs.

- *48cm x 58cm*
- **£1,795** • **Great Grooms**

Demi-Lune Card Table

- ***1837-1901***

Victorian burr walnut demi-lune card table with scrolled carved legs and feet.

- *74cm x 35cm x 43cm*
- **£1,995** • **Old Cinema**

Edwardian Occasional Tables

- ***1910***

A nest of three Edwardian occasional tables with boxwood inlay and banding and tapered straight legs.

- *55cm x 50cm*
- **£495** • **Great Grooms**

Inlaid Card Table

- ***circa 1900***

A mahogany card table with inlaid marquetry banding and medallions, on straight tapered legs.

- *72cm x 45cm*
- **£2,550** • **Great Grooms**

Expert Tips

Occasional tables are always of interest as they have such a useful function in everyday living. They can obtain high prices, especially the ones made in rare woods and with high quality inlay.

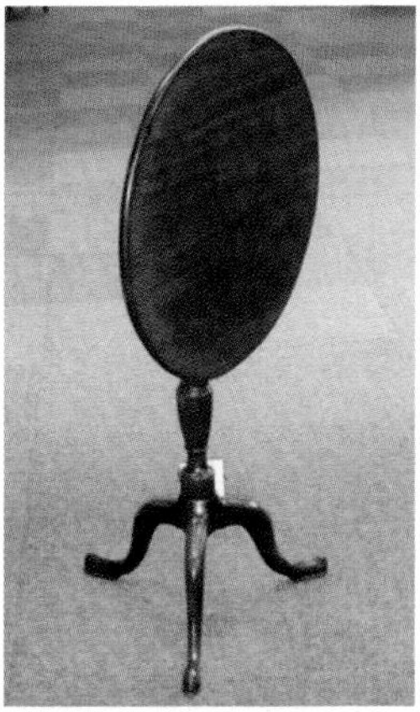

George III Tripod Table

• ***1760***
George III small circular mahogany tripod table.
• £2,950 • **Ashcombe**

Rosewood Table

• ***1860***
A rosewood occasional table, with central long drawer, two side extensions, standing on a turned stretcher with twin scrolled supports.
• *74cm x 119cm x 65cm*
• £3,250 • **Old Cinema**

Austrian Work Table

• ***early 19th century***
An early nineteenth-century olive wood work table made in Austria on stretcher base.
• *47cm x 63cm x 77cm*
• £1,150 • **N. E. McAuliffe**

Biedermeier Sofa Table

• ***circa 1820***
Swedish birchwood, Biedermeier sofa table with ebonised and gilt decoration on lion paw feet.
• *77cm x 120cm x 64cm*
• £4,500 • **R. Cavendish**

Italian Rosewood Table

• ***1900***
Italian inlaid rosewood octagonal occasional table, with circular satinwood inlay standing on eight square tapering legs.
• *72cm x 60cm*
• £900 • **Tredantiques**

Rosewood Games Table

• ***1810–20***
A Regency rosewood games table with Moroccan leather top and brass inlay and ormolu mounts.
• *height 95cm*
• £8,500 • **C.H. Major**

Regency Writing Table

• ***1810***
An excellent Regency mahogany standard end writing table on turned stretcher base.
• *height 53cm*
• £14,500 • **Ashcombe**

Victorian Drinks Table

• ***1880***
A Victorian drinks table with an Eastern influence in light oak with ebony finials on unusual legs.
• *76cm x 58cm x 43cm*
• £460 • **Myriad**

Expert Tips

Snap-top or tripod tables should have good firm bases and the table top should be constructed out of a single piece of wood.

Circular Side Table ▲

- **1890**

Small circular table on tripod base, inlaid with satinwood, box and rosewood with an inlaid knight on horseback.

- *height 74cm*
- £1,400 • **J. Fox**

Welsh Oak Table ▲

- **circa 1740**

A Welsh country-made eighteenth-century oak three drawer side table with original handles.

- *74cm x 83cm x 47cm*
- £1,850 • **Rod Wilson**

French Marquetry Table ▲

- **circa 1890**

A French centre table with shaped top with marquetry inlay and ormolu mounts on cabriole legs.

- *77cm x 152cm x 95cm*
- £8,500 • **Tredantiques**

Chinese Lacquered Table ▼

- **1800**

A pair of eighteenth-century Chinese lacquer panels inset into more recent brass frames.

- *65cm x 55cm*
- £1,750 • **C.H. Major**

Marquetry Table ▼

- **circa 1875**

French marquetry table with hinged table top with fitted interior and carved and gilded legs.

- *74cm x 81cm*
- £2,750 • **C.H. Major**

Expert Tips

It cannot be overemphasised that, when purchasing lacquer top tables, marquetry or boulle, they must be in first class condition, as damage impairs their value considerably. Ornateness within the design of the table is very desirable but when this is applied to ebony and ivory inlay this can often depress the value of these pieces.

Oval Hall Tables ▲

- **1860**

Victorian small oval top table with a basket base on cabriole legs with ceramic castors.

- *72cm x 116cm x 142cm*
- £4,500 • **J. Fox**

Mahogany Drinks Table ▲

- **1880**

A mahogany side table by Maples with silver-plated mounts and original decanters on silver plated castors.

- *97cm x 118cm x 56cm*
- £3,800 • **J. Fox**

Carved Writing Table ▲

- **1825**

A fine Regency rosewood writing or side table attributed to Gillows of Lancaster and made in 1825. The well-figured veneers to the top are complemented by exquisite gadrooned carving to the edge and it is fitted with two frieze drawers. The design for this table is included in Gillows estimates, drawings and costings book for 1826, nos 3480 & 3496.

- *75cm x 106cm x 60cm*
- £8,950 • **Freshfords**

Mahogany Side Table

• *circa 1870s*

Victorian mahogany table with leather writing top and one long single drawer on tapered turned legs with original brass castors.

• *height 70cm*

• **£595** • **Old Cinema**

Victorian Chess Table

• *1860*

A Victorian mother-of-pearl chess table by Jenning and Betteridge, with pierced fan shaped decoration to top, single turned pedestal on circular base with upturned tripod feet.

• *73cm x 49cm*

• **£1,250** • **Tredantiques**

Italian Console Table

• *1830*

A Venetian giltwood console table, with pink and white marble top, serpentine carved front, with profusely carved legs and stretcher.

• *90cm x 140cm x 46cm*

• **£1,950** • **Tredantiques**

Expert Tips

Period chess tables are always of great interest to the collector as the game of chess has a timeless appeal.

Cricket Table

• *1750*

An oak oval cricket table, on a tripod base with square, straight legs.

• *62cm x 57cm*

• **£3,600** • **Paul Hopwell**

Boulle Table

• *1880*

A magnificent circular green ebonised boulle circular table with brass inlaid decoration.

• *77cm x 138cm*

• **£8,500** • **Old Cinema**

French Circular Table

• *circa 1900*

A French circular satinwood and fruitwood table standing on square tapering legs.

• *72cm x 50cm*

• **£900** • **Tredantiques**

Spider-legged Work Table

• *1800*

Mahogany work table with unusual spider legs.

• *72cm x 53cm x 40cm*

• **£4,200** • **O.F. Wilson**

Louis XVI Table

• ***19th century***
Louis XV1-style, small mahogany table, with three tiers of drawers below a pierced brass gallery.
• *78cm x 43cm x 32cm*
• £2,600 • **O.F. Wilson**

Victorian Tea Table

• ***1860***
An English Victorian rosewood tea table, on cabriole legs with X-framed stretcher and carved finial.
• *24cm x 22cm*
• £1,585 • **Ranby Hall**

Games Table

• ***1880***
Victorian rosewood card table enclosing baize-lined interior.
• *74cm x 56cm*
• £1,695 • **The Old Cinema**

Lady's Sewing Table

• ***early 19th century***
A Regency figured mahogany inlaid lady's sewing table with a set of four drawers with ivory escutcheons, turned handles, standing on square tapered legs, with S-shaped stretcher.
• *83cm x 48cm x 37cm*
• £1,950 • **S. Duggan**

Granite-Top Table

• ***1830***
A Louis Philippe table with a granite top, on central pedestal, with heavily carved tripod base, and scrolled paw feet.
• *77cm x 100cm*
• £5,250 • **Ranby Hall**

Rosewood Work Table

• ***1840***
Rosewood Dantas work table raised on a U-shaped pedestal base.
• *72cm x 80cm x 40cm*
• £2,800 • **Midwinter**

Swedish Console Table with Griffin

• ***18th century***
Swedish giltwood console table with central carved griffin on black-figured marble plinth.
• *82cm x 75cm x 47cm*
• £8,500 • **Heytesbury**

Oak Side Table

• ***17th century***
A seventeenth-century oak side table with a single drawer on a ball-and-reel turned frame, with rich patina on ball feet.
• *68cm x 77cm x 54cm*
• £5,600 • **Peter Bunting**

Wardrobes

Linen Press

- *circa 1780*

18th-century mahogany linen press with oval door panels, oval brass mounts and moulded cornice, on splayed bracket feet.

- *height 1.6m*
- £6,800 • Chambers

Georgian Linen Press

- *circa 1830*

A mahogany linen press with moulded and cavetto cornice, two short and two full-width mahogany and pine-lined cockbeaded drawers fitted with oval brass decorations.

- *height 2.1m*
- £3,950 • J. Collins

Victorian Compactum

- *circa mid-19th century*

Mahogany compactum, comprising two hanging side cabinets, drawers and shelves.

- *height 2.5m*
- £3,750 • Old Cinema

North Breton Armoire

- *18th century*

With primitive carving, lined with 19th-century fabric.

- *height 1.6m*
- £2,400 • Angel

Oak Cupboard

- *circa 1780*

Oak cupboard with two six-panelled doors above four drawers, on bracket feet.

- *height 1.95m*
- £4,800 • Red Lion

Victorian Compactum

- *circa mid-19th century*

Mahogany compactum comprising two hanging cupboards, two linen presses and five tiers of drawers.

- *height 2.2m*
- £3,750 • Old Cinema

Walnut Armoire

- *circa 1840*

With deep carvings, a simple cornice with shell motif, ornate hinges and a shaped apron.

- *height 2.2m*
- £3,750 • Town & Country

Linen Press

- ***circa* 1780**

An 18th-century mahogany linen press with original fittings.

- *height 2.2m*
- £6,800 • Chambers

English Cupboard

- ***circa* 1780**

Very fine cupboard with secret compartments, heavily cut frieze and pilaster decoration.

- *height 2.6m*
- £12,800 • Riverbank

Jersey Wardrobe

- ***circa* 1800**

An early 19th-century mahogany wardrobe.

- *height 2.09m*
- £3,500 • Terence Morse

French Armoire

- ***circa* 1790**

A Provençale armoire with serpentine apron.

- *height 1.69m*
- £1,200 • Lynda Franklin

Dutch Linen Press

- ***circa early 19th century***

Mahogany with pilasters and gilt mounts on plinth feet.

- *height 2m*
- £4,500 • Old Cinema

Expert Tips

The size of the panels of these items render them particularly vulnerable to splitting. Beware central heating!

Elm Press

- ***circa* 1820**

English linen-press cupboard on shaped bracket feet.

- *height 1.8m*
- £2,850 • Angel

Breakfront Wardrobe

- ***circa late 19th century***

Inverted mahogany breakfront wardrobe with brass mounts, on shaped bracket feet.

- *height 2m*
- £3,995 • Old Cinema

Georgian Linen Press

- *1780*

A Georgian mahogany linen press with figured mahogany panelled doors, above three tiers of drawers with oval brass mounts.

- *110cm x 81cm*
- **£3,950** • **Old Cinema**

Expert Tips

Linen presses, which are cupboards used to store linen, date from the 1600s. A Georgian linen press was usually made from mahogany or walnut, and came with panelled doors and three tiers of drawers. The doors of early oak linen presses could be constructed with six or more panels. They come in a wide range of styles, which include the breakfronted and bowfronted examples, along with a range of sizes, as some could be huge.

Breakfront Compactum

- *circa 1830*

An English George IV flame mahogany breakfront compactum with central pediment, having panelled cupboards, and three long drawers below.

- *208cm x 226cm x 57cm*
- **£3,850** • **Ranby Hall**

Victorian Linen Press

- *circa 1860*

A fine Victorian flame mahogany linen press, with panelled doors above two short and two long drawers, enclosing an interior with sliding drawers, standing on a plinth base.

- *149cm x 129cm x 54cm*
- **£4,450** • **Ranby Hall**

Housekeeper's Cupboard

- *circa 1800*

An early nineteenth century housekeeper's cupboard with carved oak panelling, with four drawers below, standing on ogee bracket foot.

- *72cm x 134cm x 53cm*
- **£5,750** • **Rod Wilson**

Arts and Crafts Wardrobe

- *circa 1910*

Art and Crafts oak wardrobe with central mirror and one long drawer, standing on bracket feet.

- *212cm x 112cm x 55cm*
- **£975** • **Old Cinema**

Bedroom Suite

- *1875–80*

A French Second Empire-style wardrobe, being part of a bedroom set including bed, wardrobe, and two side cabinets. The wardrobe with a moulded cornice, mirrored cupboards and ormolu foliate decoration, standing on bun feet.

- *height 240cm*
- **£35,000** • **Sleeping Beauty**

Directory of Dealers

There follows a list of antique dealers, many of whom have provided items in the main body of the book and all of whom will be happy to assist within their areas of expertise.

Abacus Antiques
(ref: Abacus)
Grays Antiques Market,
58 Davies Street, London W1Y 2LP
Tel: 020 7629 9681

Antiques.

Aberg Antiques
(ref: Aberg)
42 The Little Boltons,
London SW10 9LN
Tel: 020 7370 7253
Fax: 020 7370 7253

Furniture.

Norman Adams Ltd
8–10 Hans Road,
London SW3 1RX
Tel: 020 7589 5266
Fax: 020 7589 1968
www.normanadams.com

Eighteenth-century fine English furniture, works of art, mirrors, paintings and chandeliers.

After Noah
121 Upper Street,
London N1 8ED
Tel: 020 7359 4281
Fax: 020 7359 4281
www.afternoah.com

Antique furniture, linen and postcards.

After Noah (Kings Road)
(ref: After Noah (KR))
261 Kings Road,
London SW3 5EL
Tel: 020 7351 2610
Fax: 020 7351 2610
www.afternoah.com

Antique furniture, linen and postcards.

Albany Antiques
(ref: Albany)
8–10 London Road, Hindhead,
Surrey GU26 6AF
Tel: 01428 605 528
Fax: 01428 605 528

Georgian furniture, eighteenth-century brass, Victorian antiques, porcelain and statuary.

Paul Andrews Antiques

The Furniture Court,
553 Kings Road,
London SW10 0TZ

Tel: 020 7352 4584
Fax: 020 7351 7815
www.paulandrewsantiques.co.uk

Eclectic furniture, sculpture, tapestries, paintings and works of art.

Angel Antiques
Church Street, Petworth,
West Sussex GU28 0AD
Tel: 01798 343 306
Fax: 01798 342 665

Oak, country furniture.

Antique Warehouse
9–14 Dentford Broadway,
London SE8 4PA
Tel: 020 8691 3062
Fax: 020 8691 3062
www.antiquewarehouse.co.uk

Decorative antiques.

Antiques Pavilion
175 Bermondsey Street,
London SE1 3LW
Tel: 020 7394 7856

Furniture from the Georgian period to the 1930s; also restorations.

Barham Antiques
(ref: Barham)
83 Portobello Road,
London W11 2QB
Tel: 020 7727 3845
Fax: 020 7727 3845

Victorian walnut and inlaid continental furniture, writing boxes, tea caddies, inkwells and inkstands, glass épergnes, silver plate, clocks and paintings.

Frederick Beck Ltd.
(ref: F. Beck)
22–26 Camden Passage,
Islington, London N1 8ED
Tel: 020 7226 3403
Fax: 020 7288 1305

General antiques.

Julia Bennet (Antiques)
Flemings Hill Farm,
Great Easton, Dunmow,
Essex CM6 2ER
Tel: 01279 850279

Eighteenth and early nineteenth-century furniture.

Andrew Bewick Antiques
287 Lillie Road,
London SW6 7LL
Tel: 020 7385 9025
Fax: 020 7385 9025

Decorative antiques.

Oonagh Black Antiques
(ref: Oonagh Black)
Lower Farm House, Coln Rogers,
Gloucestershire GL54 3LA
Tel: 01285 720717
Fax: 01285 720910

French and English country furniture, decorative accessories, and French science and textiles.

M. J. Bowdery
12 London Road, Hindhead,
Surrey, GU26 6AF
Tel: 01428 606376

Eighteenth and nineteenth-century furniture.

Lesley Bragge
Fairfield House, High Street,
Petworth, West Sussex
Tel: 01798 342324

Wine-related items.

I. and J. L. Brown Ltd
(ref: I. & J. L. Brown)
632–636 Kings Road,
London SW6 2DU
Tel: 020 7736 4141
Fax: 020 7736 9164
www.brownantiques.com

English country and French provincial antique and reproduction furniture.

Brown's Antique Furniture
(ref: Browns)
First Floor, The Furniture Cave,
533 Kings Road,
London SW10 0TZ
Tel: 020 7352 2046
Fax: 020 7352 6354
www.thecave.co.uk

Library and dining, and decorative objects from the early eighteenth century.

Peter Bunting Antiques
(ref: Peter Bunting)
Harthill Hall, Alport, Bakewell,
Derbyshire DE45 1LH
Tel: 01629 636203
Fax: 01629 636190

Early oak and country furniture, portraits and tapestries.

Butchoff Antiques
(ref: Butchoff)
220 Westbourne Grove,
London W11 2RH
Tel: 020 7221 8174
Fax: 020 7792 8923

English and continental furniture, decorative items, porcelain and mirrors.

Butchoff Interiors
229 Westbourne Grove,
London W11 2SE
Tel: 020 7221 8163
Fax: 020 7792 8923

One-off items, textiles, collectables, dining tables, chairs, consoles and accessories.

Canonbury Antiques Ltd
(ref: Canonbury)
174 Westbourne Grove,
London W11 2RW
Tel: 020 7229 2786
Fax: 020 7229 5840
www.canonbury-antiques.co.uk

Eighteenth and nineteenth-century furniture, reproduction furniture and accessories.

No.1 Castlegate Antiques
(ref: Castlegate)
1-3 Castlegate, Newark, Notts NG24 1AZ
Tel: 01636 701877

18th and 19th-century furniture and decorative objects.

Rupert Cavendish Antiques
(ref: R. Cavendish)
610 Kings Road,
London SW6 2DX
Tel: 020 7731 7041
Fax: 020 7731 8302
www.rupertcavendish.co.uk

European twentieth-century paintings.

Ronald G. Chambers Fine Antiques
(ref: Ronald G. Chambers)
Market Square, Petworth,
West Sussex GU28 0AH
Tel: 01798 342305
Fax: 01798 342724
www.ronaldchambers.com

Eighteenth and nineteenth-century furniture, paintings, objets d'art, clocks and jewellery.

John Clay Antiques
(ref: John Clay)
263 New Kings Road,
London SW6 4RB
Tel: 020 7731 5677

Furniture, objets d'art, silver and clocks from the eighteenth and nineteenth century.

J. Collins & Son
28 High Street, Bideford,
Devon EX39 2AN
Tel: 01237 473103
Fax: 01237 475658

Georgian and Regency furniture, Victorian oil paintings and watercolours.

Curios Gardens & Interiors
(ref: Curios)
130c Junction Road,
Tufnell Park,
London N19 5LB
Tel: 020 7272 5603
Fax: 020 7272 5603

Garden furniture, statuary, reclaimed pine furniture and antique furniture.

Michael Davidson
54 Ledbury Road,
London W11 2AJ
Tel: 020 7229 6088
Fax: 020 7792 0450

Eighteenth-century furniture, regency furniture, objects and objets d'art.

Dial Post House
Dial Post, Near Horsham,
West Sussex RH13 8NQ
Tel: 01403 713388
Fax: 01403 713388

Furniture.

Drummonds Architectural Antiques Ltd
(ref: Drummonds)
The Kirkpatrick Buildings,
25 London Road, Hindhead,
Surrey GU26 6AB
Tel: 01428 609444
Fax: 01428 609445
www.drummonds-arch.co.uk

Restored original and new bathrooms, reclaimed wood and stone flooring, fireplaces, statues, garden features, lighting, gates and railings, doors and door furniture, radiators, antique furniture, windows and large architectural features.

S. Duggan
First Floor, 533 Kings Road,
London SW10 0TZ
Tel: 020 7352 2046

Antiques.

Emanouel Corporation U.K. Ltd.
(ref: Emanouel)
64 South Audley Street,
London W1Y 5FD
Tel: 020 7493 4350
Fax: 020 7499 0996

Important antiques and fine works of art from the eighteenth and nineteenth century, and Islamic works of art.

David Ford
2 Queenstown Road, Battersea,
London SW8
Tel: 020 7622 7547

Judy Fox Antiques
(ref: J. Fox)
81 Portobello Road/
176 Westbourne Grove,
London W11
Tel: 020 7229 8130/8488
Fax: 020 7229 6998

Furniture.

Lynda Franklin

25 Charnham Street, Hungerford,
Berkshire, RG17 0EJ
Tel: 01488 682404
Fax: 01488 626089

Antiques and interior design, french furniture from the seventeenth and eighteenth centuries.

French Country Living
(ref: French Country)
Rue des Remparts,
Mougins, France
Tel: 00 33 4 93 75 53 03
Fax: 00 33 4 93 75 63 03

Antiquities and decoration.

French Room, The
5 High Street, Petworth,
West Sussex GU28 OAU
Tel: 01798 344454
Fax: 01403 269880

French period furniture and decorative wares.

Freshfords
High Street, Freshford,
Bath BA3 6EF
Tel: 01225 722111
Fax: 01225 722991
www.freshfords.com

Fine antique furniture and works of art, specialising in dining and library furniture.

Fulham Antiques
(ref: Fulham)
320 Munster Road,
London SW6 6BH
Tel: 020 7610 3644
Fax: 020 7610 3644

Antique and decorative furniture, lighting and mirrors.

Furniture Vault, The
(ref: Furniture Vault)
50 Camden Passage,
London N1 8AE
Tel: 020 7354 1047
Fax: 020 7354 1047

Eighteenth and nineteenth-century furniture.

Gabrielle de Giles
The Barn at Bilsington,
Swanton Lane, Bilsington,
Ashford, Kent TN25 7JR
Tel: 01233 720917
Fax: 01233 720156

Antique and country furniture, home interiors, designer for curtains and screens.

Great Grooms Antique Centre
(ref: Great Grooms)
Great Grooms, Parbrook,
Billinghurst, West Sussex RH14 9EU
Tel: 01403 786202
Fax: 01403 786224
www.great-grooms.co.uk

Furniture, porcelain, jewellery, silver and glass.

Guinevere Antiques Limited
(ref: Guinevere)
574–580 Kings Road,
London SW6 2DY
Tel: 020 7736 2917
Fax: 020 7736 8267

Mirrors, cabinets, lights and chandeliers.

J. de Haan & Son
(ref: J. de Haan)
PO Box 95, Newmarket,
Suffolk CB8 8ZG
Tel: 01440 821388
Fax: 01440 820410

Old English furniture, barometers, gilt mirrors and fine tea caddies.

Ross Hamilton Antiques Ltd
95 Pimlico Road,
London SW1W 8PH
Tel: 020 7730 3015
Fax: 020 7730 3015
www.lapada.uk/rosshamilton/

Seventeenth to nineteenth-century fine English and continental furniture, sixteenth to twentieth-century paintings, oriental porcelain, objets d'art and bronzes.

Harpur Deardren
First Floor, 533 Kings Road,
London SW10 0TZ
Tel: 020 7352 2046

Furniture.

Kenneth Harvey Antiques
(ref: Kenneth Harvey)
Furniture Cave,
533 Kings Road,
London SW10 0TZ
Tel: 020 7352 8645
Fax: 020 7352 3759
www.kennethharvey.com

English and French furniture, chandeliers and mirrors from the late seventeenth to twentieth century, and leather armchairs.

Victoria Harvey at Deuxieme
(ref: Victoria Harvey)
44 Church Street,
London NW8 8EP
Tel: 020 7724 0738
Fax: 020 7724 0738

General decorative antiques.

W. R. Harvey & Co. Ltd
86 Corn Street, Witney,
Oxfordshire OX8 7BU
Tel: 01993 706501
Fax: 01993 706601
www.wrharvey.co.uk

Important stock of English furniture, clocks, pictures, mirrors and works of art from 1680–1830.

Simon Hatchwell Antiques
(ref: S. Hatchwell)
533 Kings Road,
London SW10 0TZ
Tel: 020 7351 2344
Fax: 020 7351 3520

English and continental furniture, early nineteenth and twentieth-century chandeliers, lighting, bronzes, barometers and clocks, including grandfather clocks.

Gerard Hawthorn Ltd
(ref: Gerard Hawthorn)
104 Mount Street,
London W1Y 5HE
Tel: 020 7409 2888
Fax: 020 7409 2777

Chinese, Japanese and Korean ceramics and works of art.

Heytesbury Antiques
(ref: Heytesbury)
PO Box 222, Farnham,
Surrey GU10 5HN
Tel: 01252 850893

Antiques.

Paul Hopwell
(ref: Paul Hopwell)
30 High Street, West Haddon,
Northampton,
Northamptonshire NN6 7AP
Tel: 01788 510636
Fax: 01788 510044
www.antiqueoak.co.uk

Seventeenth and eighteenth-century English oak furniture.

P. L. James
590 Fulham Road,
London SW6 5NT
Tel: 020 7736 0183

Gilded mirrors, English and oriental lacquer, period objects and furniture.

L. & E. Kreckovic
559 Kings Road,
London SW6 2EB
Tel: 020 7736 0753
Fax: 020 7731 5904

Early eighteenth to nineteenth-century furniture.

Lacquer Chest, The
(ref: Lacquer Chest)
75 Kensington Church Street,
London W8 4BG
Tel: 020 7937 1306
Fax: 020 7376 0223

Military chests, china, clocks, samplers and lamps.

Lamberty
The Furniture Cave,
533 Kings Road,
London SW10 0TZ
Tel: 020 7352 3775
Fax: 020 7352 3759
www.lamberty.co.uk

M. Luther Antiques
(ref: M. Luther)
590 Kings Road, Chelsea,
London SW6 2DX
Tel: 020 7371 8492
Fax: 020 7371 8492

Eighteenth and nineteenth-century English and continental furniture, tables, chairs, mirrors and lighting.

Mac Humble Antiques
(ref: Mac Humble)
7–9 Woolley Street, Bradford on Avon,
Wiltshire BA15 1AD
Tel: 01225 866329
Fax: 01225 866329
www.machumbleantiques.co.uk

Eighteenth and nineteenth-century furniture, needlework, samplers, metalware and decorative items.

C. H. Major
154 Kensington Church Street,
London W8 4BH
Tel: 020 7229 1162
Fax: 020 7221 9676

Eighteenth and nineteenth-century English furniture.

David Martin-Taylor Antiques
(ref: D. Martin-Taylor)
558 Kings Road,
London SW6 2DZ
Tel: 020 7731 4135
Fax: 020 7371 0029
www.davidmartintaylor.com

Eighteenth and nineteenth-century continental and English furniture, objets d'art, decorative art, from the eccentric to the unusual.

Nicholas E. McAuliffe
(ref: N. E. McAuliffe)
First Floor, 533 Kings Road,
London SW10 0TZ
Tel: 020 7352 2046

Furniture.

Fiona McDonald
57 Galveston Road,
London SW15 2RZ
Tel: 020 2270 5559

Mirrors, decorative furniture and lighting.

Midwinter Antiques
(ref: Midwinter)
31 Bridge Street,
Newcastle under Lyme,
Staffordshire ST5 2RY
Tel: 01782 712483
Fax: 01630 672289

Seventeenth and eighteenth-century town and country furniture, clocks and textiles.

Mora & Upham Antiques
584 Kings Road, London SW6 2DX
Tel: 020 7731 4444
Fax: 020 7736 0440

Gilded French chairs, antique chandeliers, eighteenth and nineteenth-century English and continental furniture and mirrors.

Terence Morse & Son
(ref: T. Morse & Son)
237 Westbourne Gove,
London W11 2SE
Tel: 020 7229 4059
Fax: 020 7792 3284

Eighteenth and nineteenth-century fine English and continental furniture, linen presses and library furniture.

Myriad Antiques
(ref: Myriad)
131 Portland Road,
London W11 4LW
Tel: 020 7229 1709
Fax: 020 7221 3882

French painted furniture, garden furniture, bamboo, Victorian and Edwardian upholstered chairs, mirrors and objets d'art.

New Century
69 Kensington Church Street,
London W8 8BG
Tel: 020 7937 2410
Fax: 020 7937 2410

Design from 1860–1910.

Chris Newland Antiques
(ref: C. Newland)
30–31 Islington Green,
Lower Level, Georgian Village,
London N1 8DU
Tel: 020 7359 9805
Fax: 020 7359 9805

Furniture.

John Nicholas Antiques
First Floor, 533 Kings Road,
London SW10 0TZ
Tel: 020 7352 2046
www.thecave.co.uk

Eighteenth to twentieth-century furniture, accessories, chandeliers, lighting and tapestries.

North West Eight
(ref: North West 8)
36 Church Street,
London NW8 8EP
Tel: 020 7723 9337

Decorative antiques.

Old Cinema Antiques Warehouse, The
(ref: Old Cinema)
160 Chiswick High Road,
London W4 1PR
Tel: 020 8895 4166
Fax: 020 8995 4167
www.antiques-uk.co.uk/theoldcinema

Georgian to Art Deco furniture, large items of furniture, clocks and silver.

Old Cinema Antiques Warehouse, The
(ref: Old Cinema)
157 Tower Bridge Road,
London SE1 3LW
Tel: 020 7407 5371
Fax: 020 7403 0359
www.antiques-uk.co.uk

Victorian, Edwardian, reproduction furniture, babies' chairs, telephone boxes, and reproduction leather Chesterfields.

Old School
130c Junction Road,
Tufnell Park,
London N19
Tel: 020 7272 5603

Gardens and interiors.

Oola Boola Antiques London
(ref: Oola Boola)
166 Tower Bridge Road,
London SE1 3LS
Tel: 020 7403 0794
Fax: 020 7403 8405

Victorian, Edwardian, Art Nouveau, Art Deco, and Arts and Crafts furniture.

Fay Orton Antiques
(ref: Fay Orton)
First Floor, 533 Kings Road,
London SW10 0TZ
Tel: 020 7352 2046

Furniture.

Pillows of Bond Street
(ref: Pillows)
Bond Street,
London W11
Tel: 0468 947265

Pillows.

Pimlico Antiques
(ref: Pimlico)
Moreton Street,
London SW1
Tel: 020 7821 8448

Furniture, works of art and paintings.

Christopher Preston Ltd
(ref: C. Preston)
The Furniture Cave,
533 King's Road
London SW10 0TZ
Tel: 020 7352 4229

Antique furniture and decorative objects.

Annette Puttnam
Norton House,
Nr. Lewes, Iford,
Sussex BN7 3EJ
Tel: 01273 483366
Fax: 01273 483366

Raffety Walwyn
79 Kensington Church Street,
London W8 4BG
Tel: 020 7938 1100
Fax: 020 7938 2519
www.raffetyantiqueclocks.com

Fine antique clocks.

Ranby Hall Antiques
(ref: Ranby Hall)
Barnby Moor, Retford,
Nottingham DN22 8JQ
Tel: 01777 860696
Fax: 01777 701317
www.ranbyhall.antiques-gb.com

Antiques, decorative items and contemporary objects.

Red Lion Antiques
(ref: Red Lion)
New Street, Petworth,
West Sussex GU28 0AS
Tel: 01798 344485
Fax: 01798 342367
www.redlion-antiques.com

Seventeenth to nineteenth-century furniture.

Gordon Reece Gallery
(ref: Gordon Reece)
16 Clifford Street,
London W1X 1RG
Tel: 020 7439 0007
Fax: 020 7437 5715
www.gordonreecegalleries.com

Flat woven rugs and nomadic carpets, tribal sculpture, jewellery, furniture, decorative and non-European folk art especially ethnic and oriental ceramics.

Riverbank Gallery Ltd
(ref: Riverbank)
High Street, Petworth,
West Sussex GU28 0AU
Tel: 01798 344401
Fax: 01798 343135

Large English eighteenth and nineteenth-century furniture, decorative items, garden furniture and decorative paintings.

Sieff
49 Long Street, Tetbury,
Gloucestershire, GL8 8AA
Tel: 01666 504477
Fax: 01666 504478

Eighteenth and nineteenth-century French provincial fruitwood, and some twentieth-century furniture.

Sign of the Hygra
(ref: Hygra)
2 Middleton Road,
London E8 4BL
Tel: 020 7254 7074
Fax: 0870 125669
www.hygra.com

Boxes.

Sign of the Times
St Oswalds Mews,
London N6 2UT
Tel: 020 7584 3842
www.antiquesline.com

Furniture, decorative metalware and glass.

Sinai Antiques
219–221 Kensington Church Street,
London W8 7LX
Tel: 020 7229 6190

Antiques and works of art.

Sleeping Beauty
579–581 Kings Road,
London SW6 2DY
Tel: 020 7471 4711
Fax: 020 7471 4795
www.antiquebeds.com
Antique beds.

Solaris Antiques
(ref: Solaris)
170 Westbourne Grove,
London W11 2RW
Tel: 020 7229 8100
Fax: 020 7229 8300

Decorative antiques from France and Sweden, from all periods up to 1970s

Ian Spencer
17 Godfrey Street,
London SW3 3TA

Large desks, sets of chairs and dining tables.

June & Tony Stone
(ref: J. & T. Stone)
75 Portobello Road,
London W11 2QB
Tel: 020 7221 1121

Fine antique boxes.

Sue & Alan Thompson
(ref: S. & A. Thompson)
Highland Cottage, Broomne Hall Road,
Cold Harbout RH5 6HH
Tel: 01306 711970
Fax: 01306 711970

Objects of vertu, antique tortoiseshell items, period furniture and unusual collector's items.

Through the Looking Glass
563 Kings Road,
London SW6 2EB
Tel: 020 7736 7799
Fax: 020 7602 3678

Nineteenth-century mirrors.

Tower Bridge Antiques
(ref: Tower Bridge)
159–161 Tower Bridge Road,
London SE1 3LW
Tel: 020 7403 3660
Fax: 020 7403 6058

Town & Country Antiques
(ref: Town & Country)
88 Fulham Road,
London SW3 1HR
Tel: 020 7589 0660
Fax: 020 7823 7618
www.anthony-james.com

English furniture.

Travers Antiques
71 Bell Street,
London NW1 6SX
Tel: 020 7723 4376

Furniture and decorative items from 1820–1920.

Tredantiques
77 Hill Barton Road, Whipton,
Exeter EX1 3PW
Tel: 01392 447082
Fax: 01392 462200

Furniture.

Michael Wakelin & Helen Linfield
(ref: M.W. & H.L.)
PO Box 48, Billingshurst,
West Sussex RH14 0YZ
Tel: 01403 700004
Fax: 01403 700004

Metalware, pottery, lighting, textiles and mirrors.

Graham Walpole
The Coach House,
189 Westbourne Grove,
London W11 2SB
Tel: 020 7229 0267
Fax: 020 7727 7584

Small furniture, eighteenth and nineteenth-century dolls' houses, equestrian items, bronzes, pictures and decorative items.

Westland & Company
(ref: Westland & Co.)
St. Michael's Church,
The Clergy House,
Mark Street,
London EC2A 4ER
Tel: 020 7739 8094
Fax: 020 7729 3620
www.westland.co.uk

O. F. Wilson Ltd
(ref: O. F. Wilson)
Queen's Elm Parade, Old Church Street,
London SW3 6EJ
Tel: 020 7352 9554
Fax: 020 7351 0765

Continental furniture, French chimney pieces, English painted decorative furniture and mirrors.

Rod Wilson
Red Lion, New Street, Petworth,
West Sussex, GU28 0AS
Tel: 01798 344485
Fax: 01798 342367

Youll's Antiques
27–28 Charnham Street, Hungerford,
Berkshire RG17 0EJ
Tel: 01488 682046
Fax: 01488 684335
www.youll.com
English/French furniture from seventeenth to twentieth century, porcelain, silver and decorative items.

Index

D

E

F

Q

R

S

T

U

V

W

Y

Notes

MEASUREMENT CONVERSION CHART

This chart provides a scale of measurements converted from centimetres and metres to feet and inches.

1cm	2/5in
2cm	4/5in
3cm	1 1/10in
4cm	1 3/5in
5cm	2in
10cm	3 7/8in
15cm	5 9/10in
20cm	7 3/4in
25cm	9 4/5in
30cm	11 4/5in
40cm	1ft 3 3/4in
50cm	1ft 7 2/3in
75cm	2ft 5 1/2in
1 m	3ft 3 1/3in
1.25m	4ft 1 1/5in
1.5m	4ft 11in
1.75m	5ft 8 9/10in
2m	6ft 6 3/4in
2.25m	7ft 4 3/5in
2.5m	8ft 2 2/5in
3m	9ft 10 1/10in